Werner Lantermann
Susanne Lantermann
with Matthew M. Vriends

Cockatoos

Everything About Housing, Nutrition,
Breeding, and Health Care

Filled with Full-color
Photographs

Illustrations by
Fritz W. Köhler

BARRON'S

CONTENTS

Considerations Before Buying 5

This Is the Cockatoo 5

Considerations Before Buying a Cockatoo 7

Considerations Before Buying a Second Cockatoo 11

Cockatoos and Other Parrots 11

Cockatoos and Other Pets 11

Cockatoos and Children 11

Advice on Buying a Cockatoo 13

Where to Buy a Cockatoo 13

Choosing a Healthy Cockatoo 13

Determining Gender 14

Determining Age 14

Formalities of Purchase 15

Housing and Equipment 17

Keeping a Cockatoo Indoors 17

Equipment for Cages and Aviaries 18

Free Flight in the House 20

Open Perch or Indoor Climbing Tree 20

Keeping Cockatoos Outdoors 21

HOW-TO: Building a Bird Shelter and Flight Cage 22

Acclimation and Care 25

Taking Your Bird Home 25

Placement in an Aviary 25

Hand-Taming 26

Learning to "Talk" 26

If You Keep Two Cockatoos Indoors 27

Cleaning the Bird Shelter and the Flight Cage 27

Table of Dangers 29

HOW-TO: Care Measures for House Birds 34

Diet 37

Manufactured Diets 37

Fruit, Green Feed, Sprouted Feed 37

Animal Protein 38

Inappropriate Food 39

Rearing Feed 39

Vitamins and Minerals 42

Drinking Water 42

Correct Feeding 42

Cleanliness and Hygiene 42

Health and Illness 45

First-aid Measures 45

The Visit to the Avian Veterinarian 45

Common Illnesses 46

Cockatoo Breeding 53

Species Protection 53

Species Overpopulation 53

Prerequisites for Successful Breeding 53

Pairing 54

Brooding Period 55

Courtship and Mating 55

Egg Laying and Brooding 55

Development of the Young 58

Hand-raising 58

What to Watch Out for During Brooding 59

Understanding Cockatoos 61

How Cockatoos Live Together in Nature 61

Expected Behavior in Companion Cockatoos 62

Managing Behavior in Companion Cockatoos 66

Cockatoo Species 69

Interesting Facts About
Cockatoos 69

Frequently Kept
Cockatoo Species 70

Information 77

Index 78

CONSIDERATIONS BEFORE BUYING

This Is the Cockatoo

Cockatoo, a Malaysian word, has been said to mean "old Father" or "pincer"—the latter meaning being quite clear to anyone who has ever felt the sharp beak of a cockatoo. Yet, when properly cared for, these sociable parrots are the most lovable of all creatures, whose endless inventiveness and extraordinary playfulness enchant an ever-increasing number of cockatoo owners.

Cockatoos are different from other parrots in looks as well as in behavior:

Plumage: Their single-colored plumage, usually white or dark, bears a healthy coating of powder. Cockatoos are almost unique among birds in their possession of a mobile crest. The crests of the various species of cockatoos are said to be recumbent (curving back) or recurve (curving forward at the tip). Cockatoos also possess cheek feathers that can completely cover their beaks and ear coverts when they are erected as part of a facial display. As a result, cockatoos have the most expressive faces of any bird. Indeed, the facial display of a male Moluccan cockatoo, including crest, facial fan, and ear coverts, can be fully one half of his total body height![1]

Devotion (bonding): More than any other parrots, companion cockatoos can become so attached to an individual that separation becomes almost impossible without emotional injury to the cockatoo. That special person must pay a great deal of attention to the cockatoo every day. This requires committing much time to filling the more or less involuntary role of a partner.

Several complications can result from this bonding scenario: 1) aggression related to jealousy can result in injuries to humans; and 2) an extremely human-bonded cockatoo will get used to a cockatoo mate only with the greatest difficulty and may be incapable of reproducing.

Playfulness and Loud Cries: Almost all cockatoo species demonstrate extraordinary playfulness and inventiveness. A typical companion cockatoo improvises many games, tricks, shaking and climbing exercises, or the use of various objects as tools. Such activities are carried out all day long without interruption, except for brief rest periods, so that the birds are in almost constant motion. Cockatoos accompany their play with loud screams, which in the larger species can sometimes escalate to a deafening, prolonged shriek.

[1]Murphy, James J. *Cockatoos Are Different Because They Have Crests.* White Mt. Bird Firm, Inc., 1998.

A pair of Sulfur-crested cockatoos at play.

Beak Shape and Strength: Many cockatoo beaks can break human flesh in three places simultaneously because of dual points on the mandible (lower beak) and a single point on the maxilla (upper beak). Additionally, the enormous power of the cockatoo should not go unmentioned. Scarcely any other of the large parrot species can do as much mischief with its beak as the cockatoo. With ease it demolishes objects such as ordinary plastic food dishes, for example, not to mention the whittling away of perches. The larger cockatoos are also able to bend the bars of the ordinary parrot cage in a very short time and crack the joints. Therefore additional security is advised for cage doors. Buying a suitable, stable (and therefore, usually, expensive) cage is a prerequisite for keeping cockatoos.

Avoid cages that have a guillotine type door. The name explains it all. These doors open up and down, and if the cockatoo's activities loosen the device that holds the door open and in position it can fall on the bird and do serious damage.

Cockatoos are extremely intelligent and dexterous. Do not rely on the simple closing and locking devices that come with most cages. Add a locking device, such as the spring-loaded clips used by climbers, to be sure that your cockatoos will not open the door to the cage and investigate the rest of the house while you are away.

Ability to Mimic: Cockatoos have never been known as outstanding talkers but they are capable of speech and other forms of mimicry. Their real skills, however, are based on their intelligence. It is not unusual for a cockatoo that was a handfed baby to greet its owner with a charming "hello" or to say "good-bye" at just the right moment. Many cockatoos can be taught to dance in a rhythmic response to singing or music as well as to roller skate or even play tug o' war.

Mutual preening: Two cockatoos who get along well with one another tend to preen each other's plumage, especially in the places the birds can't reach by themselves.

Considerations Before Buying a Cockatoo

When you've become somewhat familiar with the cockatoo's character traits and decide that keeping one might be possible, think carefully about the following points:

✔ Companion cockatoos require a great deal of attention. The ever more intense animal-human relationship generates a time-consuming and unpredictable responsibility, which some people are not able to handle over the long term.

✔ For feeding a single cockatoo, plan on spending an average of 20 to 30 minutes per day. This involves preparing the food, cleaning the feed dishes and the cage surroundings inside the house, as well as daily dusting, for cockatoos regularly produce feather dust.

✔ The loud voice of a cockatoo can lead to difficulties, especially if you live in an apartment. Find out ahead of time if your neighbors can comfortably tolerate a parrot being kept nearby. Don't forget to tell them that some cockatoos scream even in the dark, a characteristic that is almost unheard-of in other parrots.

✔ During vacation or in case you are ill, the cockatoo should be cared for by someone it already knows. You must plan ahead for this.

✔ The cost of buying a fully-weaned cockatoo, proper medical care, and the proper equipment for keeping one can be quite expensive.

✔ Unless you have had experience in hand-feeding a baby parrot do not consider purchasing an unweaned cockatoo. There is danger to the baby bird if you are not capable of feeding it successfully enough to fill its crop at regular intervals with food of the proper consistency

TIP

Imitation Is the Highest Form of Flattery

Chi-Chi is a large umbrella cockatoo who lives with a mature couple. As there are no children in the home, both Lonnie and Anja spend a great deal of time with Chi-Chi. Some afternoons, the bird is allowed to join Lonnie as he plies his woodworking hobby in the garage. Chi-Chi watches from the safety of a Plexiglas cage while Lonnie works with power tools: saws, drills, and sanders.

One afternoon they all took a break, removing the bird from the Plexiglas enclosure, as the couple shared iced tea. The bird hopped blissfully from arm to bench to table to saw, at one point picking up a small block of wood. As Lonnie and Anja watched, Chi-Chi carefully applied the wooden block to the circular blade of the table saw, as he had seen Lonnie do so many times. The bird eyeballed the blade with interest and obvious disappointment as nothing happened. Chi-Chi reapplied the block of wood to the blade, and again seeing no result, resorted to the traditional means of reshaping wood. He simply chewed the block to splinters.

and at the proper temperature. Of course, there are great rewards if you do complete hand-feeding a baby cockatoo as it will bond with you for life and consider you to be the equivalent of its parent.

These Bare-eyed cockatoos seem to be getting along well.

The Rose-breasted cockatoo.

What Does a Companion Cockatoo Really Need?

Before you decide to purchase a companion cockatoo, it is important to realize what it will need. The following is a description of the two basics:

I. Education

A successful companion cockatoo must learn:

✔ *Appropriate Interactive Behavior.* Cockatoos are famously interactive, but many of them prefer cuddling, cuddling, or cuddling. They are capable of demanding this preference in extremely obtrusive ways, perhaps screaming for attention, perhaps biting when being picked up or put down. Successful companion cockatoos must be guided to develop routine and predictable cooperative interactions, including step-ups, playing peek-a-boo, and retiring peacefully for the evening.

✔ *Independent Behavior.* Failure to develop independent behaviors can be devastating to a cockatoo's successful long-term adjustment in companion settings. A cockatoo that does not learn to play happily alone with toys, chew wood, or disassemble puzzles might instead spend time playing with or chewing its own feathers, or jangling human nerves and eardrums with attention-demanding calls.

II. Accommodation

A successful companion cockatoo must have:

✔ *A Rich, Stimulating Environment, Including Quality Diet, Equipment, and Housing.* Cockatoos require exceptionally strong cages and an ever-changing variety of interesting toys. They need a well-planned and delivered diet and perches in diverse sizes and textures. Like other parrots, cockatoos need full spectrum lighting and access to fresh water for drinking and bathing.

✔ *Clean Quarters.* Healthy cockatoos produce lots of powder and need to be able to reduce wood and other destructible chewables to small splinters. During warm weather, they shed and replace feathers almost continuously. Cockatoos like to throw things; they often store and soak things in their water bowls; and they must, of course, poop. Optimum health and behavior are best retained in well-maintained environments, so cockatoos must live with industrious and accommodating humans who are willing to clean up after them.

✔ *Tolerant Humans.* Cockatoos are darling but demanding. Successful cockatoo families must be able to accommodate a little screaming every now and again; a little nipping, sometimes; and occasional demolition of human possessions. A happy cockatoo will be exploratory and curious, and will wish to communicate a wide variety of wonderful discoveries and emotions to treasured humans. Successful cockatoo families are loving and accepting, for cockatoos are not unlike toddlers who never grow up.

Considerations Before Buying a Second Cockatoo

Sometimes a cockatoo does not adjust well to a particular environment without the presence of another cockatoo. This need for "cockatoo-specific culture" can be addressed by the addition of another cockatoo. Two cockatoos who get along well together make fewer demands on the keeper's time because they are not so dependent on the keeper's attention as a single bird would be.

The burden of noise will naturally be much greater when you have more than one bird. Especially if you are keeping cockatoos in an outdoor aviary, their cries can lead to trouble with noise-sensitive neighbors.

The daily time needed for cleaning and care increases with two birds. The time expenditure for preparing food can be even greater if you want to breed cockatoos (see page 53).

Keeping more than two cockatoos is especially interesting for the cockatoo fancier who has breeding in mind. In this case, the construction of a bird room or an aviary and bird shelter (page 22) is recommended.

Cockatoos and Other Parrots

Other Parrots of the Same Size: Cockatoos usually get along fairly well with other parrots of the same size if there are enough opportunities for freedom of movement inside the cage or aviary. However, you should never add a third bird to an already established pair of cockatoos. It would most likely be harassed by the male, chased, and sooner or later would have to be separated from the pair.

Smaller Parakeets and Parrot Species: We do not consider such combinations advisable.

The smaller psittacines are apt to quickly fall prey to the strong beak of the cockatoo.

Cockatoos and Other Pets

Dogs and Cats: In some cases cockatoos get along well with these other pets, if both parties are allowed gradually to get used to each other. Cats, for example, after one uncomfortable encounter with the strong cockatoo beak, often make a wide circuit around a parrot cage. However, harmonious relationships among dogs, cats, and large parrots are occasionally cited in newspapers. You have to try to see what works and what doesn't in your own situation. Some dogs and most ferrets can be too predatory to safely interact with a cockatoo.

Other Small Pets: Direct contact with cockatoos frequently ends in fatality for small mammals like guinea pigs, hamsters, or mice. Smaller birds like zebra finches or canaries will also quickly fall prey to a cockatoo.

Cockatoos and Children

Babies and small children must never be left alone with a cockatoo that has the freedom of the house. If a baby competes for what was once the cockatoo's position as favorite, the bird may react with jealousy, attacking the child.

Older children and teenagers, however, can gradually become familiar with the habits of a cockatoo. At the same time they can also learn how to assume responsibility for a companion parrot, which requires regular care and feeding and must never be neglected.

ADVICE ON BUYING A COCKATOO

Where to Buy a Cockatoo

Pet Shop or Breeder: If you are a first-time parrot keeper, it's a good idea to get your cockatoo from a well-respected source such as a breeder or pet store with a good reputation for supplying healthy, well-adjusted chicks. No cockatoos have been imported into the United States since 1992, so all baby cockatoos sold legally in the United States since that time were hatched in captivity. Expect a premium, fully-weaned, handfed baby cockatoo from a primary source to be expensive—it's worth it! Some bird fanciers have breeding pairs of birds that produce lovely and healthy baby cockatoos, but the breeder chooses not to hand feed them because of the amount of work involved. When you go to purchase a baby cockatoo make sure that it has been hand fed by the breeder rather than having been left in the cage with its parents. A cockatoo baby that is not hand fed will not be tame when you get it.

Newspaper Advertisements: A more experienced cockatoo buyer may find success buying a "resale" bird from the newspaper. A young cockatoo (under four years old) that has had only one home may still be a premium prospect as a companion cockatoo. Unfortunately, some resale cockatoos have suffered "behavioral

The Sulfur-crested cockatoo.

damage" as a result of being poorly socialized, unsocialized, neglected, or otherwise abused.

Sanctuaries: Sometimes an inquiry at a sanctuary is worthwhile, because discarded cockatoos often wind up there. However, a great deal of patience and love may be required to live happily with a cockatoo that has failed in more than one home.

Choosing a Healthy Cockatoo

Proper evaluation of a cockatoo's health is impossible for a layperson, and no cockatoo should be purchased without being examined by an experienced avian veterinarian, either before or after the sale.

The following checklist may help you in evaluating a bird while making your selection:

Housing: Cages and aviaries with thick layers of droppings, dirty interior fittings, feeding dishes containing rancid food or inadequate diets, and dirty drinking water may be prime evidence of poor bird care. Poor care can easily affect the health and disposition of cockatoo chicks.

Appearance of the birds: Look for a baby cockatoo that is still handfeeding. Handfeeding babies may have a few soiled feathers, but if plumage is grown in, it should be uniform, symmetrical, and intact. If feathers are not yet opened, look for sharply pointed spikes rather than rounded unopened feathers, which may be an indication of severe, incurable, and contagious disease (Psittacine Beak and Feather Disease, also called PBFD). Baby cockatoos will have black eyes and soft, almost flexible beaks.

A healthy, fully-weaned juvenile or adult cockatoo will have powder on the feathers. Rubbing the crest or other large feathers between thumb and forefinger should leave a slick powder coating on the fingers. Nostrils should be dry and clear. Eyes should be round (not slitted), clear, and shining. Generally a sick cockatoo has an apathetic, distressed appearance. It sleeps a great deal, rests on both legs—in contrast to a healthy (adult) bird and takes little or no nourishment. Missing claws or missing toes are beauty flaws, not signs of illness, which occur rarely in handfed domestic cockatoos. A cockatoo purchased for breeding should have a complete set of claws. A cockatoo that lacks a full set of claws will not be able to remain steady on the perch during copulation. This will inhibit the bird's ability to successfully engage in breeding.

Droppings: The droppings of a healthy bird consist of olive green and white urates, and should be medium firm and formed. Unformed, watery, different-colored, or even bloody stool can be an indication of illness.

Behavior: During the brief buying encounter, it's hardly possible to tell whether a cockatoo has potential for behavioral maladjustment. Almost all baby cockatoos are cuddly and snuggly, and so a bird's potential to develop behavior problems cannot usually be determined. However, excessively noisy begging or obvious fearfulness can be a sign of potential behavioral problems in handfeeding baby cockatoos.

Determining Gender

In a few of the white cockatoo species, gender can be easily determined in mature birds. Of the species discussed in this book, the females of the Lesser Sulphur-crested, Greater Sulphur-crested, and Umbrella cockatoos can display a brown, chestnut-brown, or red-brown iris color. The iris of the mature male cockatoo of these species is dark brown to black.

Laparascopic surgical sexing is still sometimes performed by experienced veterinarians if there is some question about a bird's internal condition. DNA analysis is the best, the least invasive, most dependable scientific technique for determining gender. This procedure can be done with a mail-in kit with samples of blood feathers or a few drops of blood from a toenail.

Determining Age

Cockatoos are among the longest lived of the parrots. Although there are stories of cockatoos living for more than one hundred years, these are always poorly documented and generally result from some member of the family forgetting that a new bird was purchased when the old one died at the ripe old age of 40 or 50 years. A cockatoo that is properly fed and given plenty of exercise can easily reach 50 to 60 years of age.

The plumage of the old bird has all the typical markings (see species descriptions, page 69). In young birds, the yellow cheek patch, for example, or the yellow crest color (in Lesser and Greater Sulphur-crested cockatoos) is paler. The plumage of young Rose-breasted cockatoos is duller all over. Young Greater Sulphur-crested cockatoos and Umbrella-crested cockatoos often show pale gray shadows in the plumage. In young Philippine Red-vented cockatoos the tail feathers are salmon-colored and become red only with age.

The iris color undergoes a color change over the course of several months and years. In adult female cockatoos, the iris is usually intense red or red-brown in color, whereas in birds under two years old, as a rule, it is dark brown or yellow-brown.

The beak of a young bird is shiny and smooth, and without the visible stratifications that develop with the growth of horn in older parrots.

The feet of younger cockatoos display a somewhat more widely spread scale structure.

In the first weeks of life, young birds rest on both feet and only later adopt the typical one-legged sleeping and resting position.

Formalities of Purchase

When buying a cockatoo, various legal regulations must be observed. The overall guiding principle is the Washington agreement, the Convention on International Trade in Endangered Species (CITES) of Wild Flora and Fauna (hereafter referred to as WA), which comprehensively lists all animal and plant species that are threatened, endangered, or threatened with extinction. The agreement is divided into three categories (Appendices I through III). All cockatoo species (with the exception of the Palm cockatoo, which is listed in Appendix I and is one of the animal species threatened with extinction) are entered in Appendix II of the WA, which lists those species that are under special regulation but that may still be bought and sold. Of course, wild-caught birds may not be imported into the United States.

Leg Band: The band is the legal identification for the bird. It helps to document transfers of ownership as well as proof of ownership, when necessary.

Sales Contract: Some states require that the sale of a psittacine bird be documented and reported to the state agency tracking parrot sales. Additionally, most sales contracts specify length and details of health guarantees as well as documenting age and, in some cases, parentage of the birds.

HOUSING AND EQUIPMENT

Keeping a Cockatoo Indoors

Indoor Cage Size: Because they are so active, the small companion cockatoos need just as just as much cage space as the larger ones. For a single bird or for temporary accommodation of a pair, the cage must have a floor surface area of at least 27 × 27 inches (70 × 70 cm, and a height of 39 inches (100 cm). Breeding cages are probably best set up as flights that are longer—at least 4 to 6 feet (120 to 180 cm)—rather than taller.

Cage Shape: A companion parrot cage should be square, with a right-angled base; round cages are unsuitable.

Bars: At least two sides of the cage bars should be horizontal so that the cockatoo can climb readily, and the gauge should be heavy enough so that the bird can't bend the bars with its strong beak.

Tray: Commercially available parrot cages have trays for catching droppings that can be pulled out like a drawer. If the bird can get to the tray, it's better off made with galvanized steel.

An Umbrella cockatoo having some lunch.

Cage Door: The cage door should be large enough so that the parrot can go in and out easily on a human hand, without having to lower the crest. Some cockatoos learn very quickly how to open the cage door with their beaks, so it is advisable to secure the door with a snap hook and lock.

The Bird Room

A bird room is almost the ideal setup for keeping cockatoos. For this you need an empty room with windows, in which the cockatoos can move freely without any cage boundaries.

However, such a room needs careful preparation to make it suitable for cockatoos:

✔ All carpets, wall and ceiling coverings must be removed.

✔ Walls and ceiling must be covered with a nontoxic coat of whitewash or latex paint (available from a paint dealer), or be tiled.

✔ Doors, heating units, exposed electrical wires, electrical outlets, light switches, and light fixtures should be covered with tin or wire mesh.

✔ It is a good idea to seal the floor so that no dampness can seep through to rooms underneath.

✔ Wooden floors or carpeted floors should be converted to tile.

✔ The amount of equipment needed depends on the number of birds: climbing trees (see page 20), bathing pans, a feeding board with removable dishes, and nest boxes (page 19).

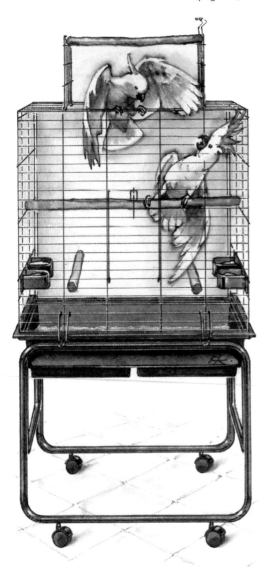

Advantages of this type of room include:
✔ The cockatoos live in a controlled, evenly maintained climate.
✔ The loud voices of the cockatoos are not so audible to neighbors living nearby.
✔ There is less danger of theft.
Disadvantages include:
✔ The parrots receive only a limited amount of daylight.
✔ Full spectrum lighting must be provided.
✔ "Rainfall" in the form of daily showers must be provided.

Equipment for Cages and Aviaries

Perches: Use round perches with a diameter of about 1 inch (25 to 30 mm) for smaller cockatoos (see description of species, page 69); for larger species the diameter should be 1½ to 2 inches (35 to 45 mm). It's good to have the perches of varying thicknesses so that muscles are exercised and the birds' feet don't go lame. The branches of unsprayed fruit trees (after being carefully scrubbed under hot running water) make excellent perches. Their rough upper surfaces are good for wearing down the claws of the cockatoos by natural means, as well as for foot exercises. Perches need to be mounted in the cage so that the bowls for water and food will not be fouled by the falling droppings of the birds.

Food and Water Dishes: When you buy a parrot cage, ordinary plastic food and water bowls are usually included. Plastic dishes will

A parrot cage with an outside perch. You can keep two of the smaller cockatoo species in a cage like this if they are allowed to fly every day.

Exercise equipment, like this large-link chain, climbing ropes, or fresh branches are important for the caged cockatoo.

be gnawed to pieces by the cockatoos in a short time and must then be changed. Better food and water dishes are those made of pottery or stainless steel, which can be fastened in the cage, aviary, or bird room with special holders (all available from the pet dealer). There should be a total of three dishes (see page 42).

Bathing Pans: Cockatoos like to bathe to get rid of feather dust. Shallow clay flowerpot saucers with a diameter of 12 to 14 inches (30 to 35 cm) are excellent for this purpose.

Play and Exercise Equipment: Chains with large links, climbing ropes, fresh branches for gnawing, and wooden parrot toys present the single bird as well as aviary birds with opportunities to exercise and provide variety in their caged existence; they also serve to maintain the condition of beak and claws.

Caution: Do not use any branches from poisonous trees or shrubs! For example, acacia, apple, cherry, yew, laburnum, viburnum, black honeysuckle, holly, dwarf elder, and many evergreens are all poisonous.

Calcium Block: It's pointless to put a calcium block into some cockatoo cages. The birds will peck it to pieces within minutes and throw it on the floor. The remains are then ignored completely. Since the advent of modern scientifically formulated diets, we no longer need to add vitamins and minerals to our bird's diets at all unless the veterinaran detects a special condition requiring supplementation.

Substratum: In recent years, Dr. Susan Clubb, an avian veterinarian from Florida, has reported university studies that demonstrate that newspaper with print is the best material tested to line the bottom of bird cages. She reports that the ink in the newspaper appears to retard the growth of bacteria, fungus, and molds more than any other material tested.

Nest Boxes: If you want to breed parrots, you should make arrangements ahead of time so that you can introduce a nest box (see Prerequisites for Successful Breeding, page 53) into an aviary or a bird room and be able to check it.

Placement of Cage or Aviary: Choose a quiet corner of the living area that is easily seen from most areas of the living area so that the cockatoo can take part in the life of the family and will not become bored. Never put the cage directly on the floor. This makes the cockatoo feel insecure. Many domestic companion cockatoos develop territorial behaviors if they are housed high, and may bite humans that are shorter than they. It's best to house

a companion domestic cockatoo no higher than the height of the shortest person. In homes where children or very short adults are present, a small stepladder can assist even the shortest family member in retrieving a well-socialized cockatoo from the top of the cage.

Free Flight in the House

Freedom to fly about the house is especially dangerous for cockatoos. While it offers excitement and opportunity for exercise, it is generally considered too dangerous in these days of ceiling fans and many-tentacled electrical appliances. Companion parrots should be safely and sensitively groomed to prevent indoor flight (see page 34).

Caution: Remove all houseplants so that the cockatoo can't nibble or eat them. Otherwise poisoning and death might result.

This climbing tree, firmly fastened in a cement pot filled with sand, consists of a well-branched natural limb to which perches have been added.

Open Perch or Indoor Climbing Tree

Under supervision, hand-tame cockatoos can be kept during the day for hours at a time on a free perch or climbing tree. It's a pleasant change for the cockatoo, and the keeper can then enjoy watching the acrobatic skills of his bird. The parrot should spend the rest of the time in its cage and it should be fed there. In time, the bird develops a regular daily rhythm. Eventually it will return voluntarily to its cage with hunger and the onset of darkness. lame, wing-feather-trimmed cockatoos enjoy daily transportation to and from the cage as a guaranteed amount of human attention they will receive.

Open Perch: The simplest form of open perch indoors is one that is fastened onto the top of the cage. It should be mounted approximately 6 inches (15 cm) above the roof and should not extend to the side beyond the cage measurements, so that the bird droppings will fall into the cage and not onto the floor. The opportunities for the cockatoo to exercise on such a perch are quite limited, however.

Climbing Tree: For a climbing tree you need a flowerpot filled with sand or a cement pot (diameter about 39 inches [100 cm]; height about 7½ inches [50 cm]) and a well-branched limb. To keep the branch upright in the container, dampen the sand somewhat before you put it in the container and then tamp it down well. Of course you can also purchase suitable climbing trees in many pet stores. The more chances to climb the tree offers, the better for the cockatoo.

A Bare-eyed cockatoo in his climbing tree.

Warning: Improperly fastened perches or ones that break suddenly can injure the bird or even kill it with a fall.

Keeping Cockatoos Outdoors

A bird shelter with a garden flight cage attached offers the cockatoos the best possible quality of life they can enjoy in human captivity.

The parrots have light, air, sun, rain, and opportunities to dig, fly, or climb. If you plan to allow breeding and to keep several cockatoos, this form of housing or a bird room is highly recommended.

Your building plans must allow for several basic considerations:

✔ Find out about local building regulations and whether a building permit is necessary.

✔ Use only very strong construction materials, ones that can stand up under the strong beaks of the cockatoos.

✔ The bird shelter should be built of brick or stone and sit on a solid cement foundation. Good insulation saves on heating.

✔ The use of simple transparent glass bricks for windows is ideal.

✔ The fly-through to the flight cage is created with a glass-brick-equipped aluminum swivel window (size about 19½ × 9¾ inches [50 × 25 cm]).

✔ Ceramic tiles are particularly good for covering the walls and floor because they are easy to clean and can't be easily destroyed by cockatoo beaks.

✔ Heating, light (fluorescents), and running water are essential features for the bird shelter.

✔ The size of the inside space: a floor surface of

72 × 24 inches (186 × 62 cm) and 48 inches (124 cm) in height is enough for a pair of cockatoos.

✔ The equipment for the interior consists of a feeding board with removable dishes, several perches, and a nest box.

Note: Besides conforming to code requirements, the proposed aviary and bird shelter should be approved as to their suitability for proper maintenance of the birds.

The flight cage should be attached to the shelter so that the cockatoos can leave their inner room even in bad weather. The following points must be considered when you are building the flight cage:

✔ It is advisable to lay a cement foundation (being careful to observe building codes).

✔ If you are handy with tools you can make the cage supports yourself from galvanized steel pipes (bolted or welded).

✔ It's best to use galvanized wire mesh for fencing. Mesh size of 0.8 × 0.8 inches (19 × 19 mm) and wire gauge of 0.04 to 0.06 inches (1.05 to 1.50 mm) will do for small cockatoos; for larger birds use mesh size of 2 × 2 inches (50 × 50 mm) and wire gauge of 0.16 inches (4 mm).

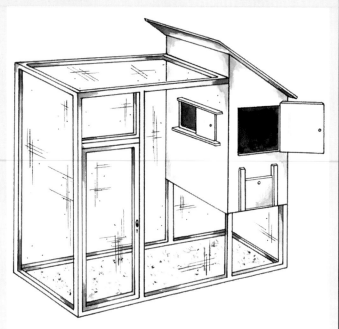

A sample of a smaller, wooden cockatoo shelter.

An outdoor aviary with four flights and shelters.

✔ Rats, mice, and other small mammals carry disease or even kill cockatoos if they get into the aviary. Therefore, be sure to secure the fencing with a small enough mesh size.

✔ A third of the flight should be roofed to offer the cockatoos shelter from too much rain or sun.

✔ Paving flags are especially good for the flight cage floor. Many cockatoos like to scratch and dig in the ground; you can add a thick layer of sand.

✔ For the entrance to the flight cage, it is recommended that you make a small outer door that is secured, and allow a space and a second door, like an air lock, to keep the cockatoos from escaping.

✔ The equipment for the aviary consists of climbing trees, baths, and several perches (see page 20).

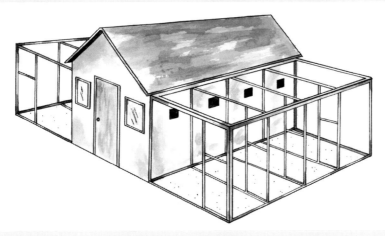

An outdoor aviary consisting of eight single-pair flights: an excellent setup for breeding various cockatoo species.

ACCLIMATION AND CARE

Taking Your Bird Home

After you're neonatal (unweaned) cockatoo becomes a juvenile or fully weaned bird, you can take it home safely in a car in a rigid carrier. The bird should not be loose in the car, as this can lead to car accidents. Even the most inconsequential accident that doesn't injure humans can easily injure a loose bird in the car.

Ideally, the cage the bird has been in should be taken home, or one identical to it should await the bird, fully furnished in the new home. Try to bring the baby home early in the day, so that it has time to become accustomed to its cage in the new surroundings. A very young (under six months old) cockatoo might prefer to spend the night in the carrier, rather than be introduced to an unfamiliar cage late in the day.

You will have a window of opportunity of two days to six months during which an exuberant young cockatoo will willingly cooperate with patterning exercises such as step-up and towel peek-a-boo's. During this same time period, a young cockatoo must also learn independent play habits.

During this period you should:

✔ Provide the cockatoo with peace and give it time to get to know its new environment.

Two Sulfur-crested cockatoos lean in for a kiss.

✔ Keep visitors and resident pets well away from it.

✔ Maintain the recommended diet from the person from whom the bird was purchased, or correct the diet (see Diet, page 37).

✔ Take the bird, as quickly as possible, to an experienced avian veterinarian for an examination and blood tests to verify the bird's health.

✔ Practice stepping the bird from hand to hand to pattern cooperation.

✔ Play peek-a-boo in a towel to get the bird used to restraint for grooming and examinations.

✔ Observe the bird's behavior to ensure that it is interested and lively and develops natural curiosity rather than focusing on one person and his attentions.

✔ Provide a variety of toys as tools for the development of independent play behaviors. Play with the toys to demonstrate how they can be used.

Placement in an Aviary

A cockatoo that is intended for an aviary is always first introduced into the bird shelter. Such a bird should have full wings and flight capacity. If possible, first place the parrot in a separate section inside the shelter so that it can get comfortable with its new surroundings. With a mature cockatoo, particularly, great care must be taken to integrate the bird into an already established aviary community. The connecting hatch to the flight cage should not be opened until a cockatoo has become familiar with the dimensions of the bird shelter, finds the perches without great difficulty, and regularly visits the feeding dish.

Some birds must be placed in the flight cage and brought back into the shelter again before they learn to find the way by themselves.

Hand-taming

Hand-tame describes a parrot that willingly steps up, without biting, onto your hand upon request. To achieve and maintain this requires practice in a happy, cooperative interaction. A newly-weaned juvenile cockatoo should enjoy practicing the step-up routine for at least a minute or two on most days. The bird's enjoyment of the interaction is the most important part.

While a very young cockatoo will probably willingly cooperate almost anyplace with anything involving touch, you might have to begin step-up practice with an older bird in unfamiliar territory. A laundry room or hallway is usually perfect, as the bird will probably never spend much time in these areas, and therefore should not develop territorial behavior in them. Step-up practice should include practice stepping the bird from the hand to and from an unfamiliar perch, practice stepping the bird from hand to hand, practice stepping the bird from a hand-held perch to and from an unfamiliar perch, practice stepping the bird from a hand-held perch to a hand-held perch, and practice stepping the bird from a familiar perch to and from both hands and to and from hand-held perches.

Be sure to offer affection and praise after each completed step-up. Always discontinue step-up practice only after a successful completion of the command. This is crucial to good patterning. If the command is not successful, alter technique, approach, or prompting mannerisms rather than continue with unsuccessful methods. Be careful not to reinforce unsuccessful patterns.

There is no substitute for warm, genuine human enthusiasm as a reward for the bird's success in stepping up. Especially with shy or cautious birds, the bird's enjoyment of the process is essential. If the bird is not eagerly, or at least willingly, cooperating with step-ups and step-up practice, something is going wrong, and the owner should find professional help immediately.

Intensive contact with humans is extremely important for the single bird because the cockatoo has a great need for social contact (for a partner). With the onset of sexual maturity this need becomes even stronger. Without appropriate behavioral training to be both interactive and independent, a neglected cockatoo can easily respond by beginning to scream, or pulling out its feathers.

Learning to "Talk"

Speaking, or more correctly, the imitation of human words is, for parrots, a form of making contact with their caretakers. All large parrots possess the ability (some more, some less) to imitate words or various sounds. In general, cockatoos do not master this skill to a high degree, but through patient schooling you can eventually succeed in training any cockatoo to produce one or another word or short phrases. Vowels (a, e, i, o, u) usually can be imitated better than consonants or sibilants.

If You Keep Two Cockatoos Indoors

Some people believe that keeping a pair of cockatoos that are bonded to each other rather than to humans is easier than keeping just one cockatoo. The jury is still out on that one. Usually a cockatoo owner already has one bird before deciding to get a second. Of course it isn't entirely easy to bring two strange parrots together. Be sure to choose a bird of the opposite sex (see Determining Gender, page 14) of the same cockatoo species or subspecies. Many times you may thus get a harmonious pair that may even breed in the right circumstances. It's rarely a good idea to pair up two cockatoos of the same sex, or different species.

Getting Used to Each Other: Never put two strange birds together right off. First the cockatoos should observe and get to know each other—separated by a cage wall—for several days or weeks. Only then do you bring both parrots together on neutral ground, that is, not in the cage of the established bird, and observe their behavior. If the pair is compatible, the mood of the cockatoos is easy to determine by the fanning of the tail or the erection of the crest (see Courtship Behavior, page 55). If the meeting continues without any disturbances, they may remain together in the same cage; otherwise they should be separated and the attempt repeated later until both birds come to an agreement. This should not take more than three or four attempts. If it does, you may want to reconsider the match.

Note: A single bird loses a little of its original tameness as it turns more to its mate than to its caretaker. Pairs that get along well together can often be left completely alone, because they can keep each other occupied.

TIP

Clutzy Cockatoos

Because of their curious natures and excellent mechanical ability, cockatoos are notoriously difficult to train to stay put and are famous as escape artists. Combine those attributes with the ability to fly and you have a creature that can be exceptionally accident-prone. Stories of hanged, electrocuted, and escaped cockatoos abound.

More than one experienced avian veterinarian has been heard to say, if it's been in an accident, it's probably a cockatoo!

Cleaning the Bird Shelter and the Flight Cage

Daily: Remove leftover food; clean feed and water dishes with hot water, dry, and refill.

Weekly: Rake out earth and sand substrate and, if necessary, spread a layer of clean sand.

Monthly: The perches will be gnawed away relatively quickly by the cockatoos' strong beaks. Thus, regular changing of perches is required. Storing natural branches is advisable.

Every Six Months: Completely change the floor litter; scrub the floor of the flight cage, disinfect, and spread with a layer of clean sand.

Yearly: Major cleaning; wash down even the flight caging and the walls of the bird shelter. If necessary, apply a new layer of paint.

Important: During the cleaning and disinfection, the parrots must be removed to another place and returned to the aviary when the shelter is dry.

An owner getting to know her Umbrella cockatoo.

A five-week-old Eleanora cockatoo.

Table of Dangers

Source of Danger	Consequences	How to Avoid
Adhesives	Poisoning with fatal outcome caused by volatile solvents.	Remove all animals from the room when using adhesives (repairing, model-making, laying floors) and ventilate very well after the work is finished.
Bathroom	Escaping through opened window. Drowning by falling into open toilet, sink, or tub. Poisoning from cleaning materials and chemicals.	Keep parrots out of the bathroom; never leave the bathroom door open. Maintain wing-feather trims and teach the bird to stay in bird-proofed areas.
Cage Wire	Strangling or getting stuck in grill with openings that are too large. Injuries to toes and head on thin, sharp-edged wire.	Choose a mesh size and a wire gauge that are appropriate for the size of the bird and examine the cage regularly for loose parts and changes caused by the bird and use over time.
Ceiling fans	Birds allowed to fly indoors crash into spinning blades.	Install protective grill or shield access to fan. Maintain wing-feather trims and teach the bird to stay in bird-proofed areas.
Doors	Caught or crushed in a carelessly closed or opened door. Escaping.	Accidents and escape can be avoided only with the greatest vigilance. Maintain wing-feather trims and teach the bird to stay in bird-proofed areas.
Drafts	Colds.	Avoid drafts as much as possible; set up a windbreak in an outdoor aviary.
Electric wires	Shock from gnawing or biting through wires; often fatal.	Conceal wires under trim and carpets and behind furniture, or cover with metal shields; pull plugs. Maintain wing-feather trims and teach the bird to stay in bird-proofed areas.

Table of Dangers (continued)

Source of Danger	Consequences	How to Avoid
Kitchen	Steam can seriously injure and fumes (especially burning plastics) can kill birds. Burns from hot burners and hot food in open containers.	Don't keep the bird in the kitchen, or else ventilate it regularly. Be careful, however, that there are no drafts. Do not leave hot burners or pots uncovered. Maintain wing-feather trims and teach the bird to stay in bird-proofed areas.
Large parrots (in an aviary)	Fighting and wounds; fatal in exceptional cases.	Never leave birds of different large species together unsupervised.
Other birds (rivals)	Fierce fighting. Development of stress; promotion of psychological illness.	Carefully introduce birds to other birds in the aviary and observe them until a pattern of dominance, which is tolerable for all birds, has evolved.
Predatory pets (dogs, cats, and ferrets)	Fighting and wounds; fatal in exceptional cases.	Never allow unknown animals in the vicinity of the birds or the aviary. If a bird's skin has been punctured by the teeth or claws of a mammal, take it immediately to an avian veterinarian for preventive antibiotic therapy.
Plate glass	Flying against it, resulting in concussion or broken neck.	Cover plate glass (windows, balcony doors, glass walls) with curtains or accustom the parrot to what is for it invisible room boundaries: lower shades to two thirds, increase the uncovered surface a bit each day. Maintain wing-feather trims and teach the bird to stay in bird-proofed areas.
Sharp objects (wires, nails, wood splinters)	Wounds, punctures, swallowing.	Don't leave anything lying around; be careful when building cages and attaching fencing for the aviary not to let any nails protrude.

Table of Dangers (continued)

Source of Danger	Consequences	How to Avoid
Poisons	Potentially lethal disturbances by tin, verdigris, nicotine, mercury, plastic-coated cookware, adhesives, cleaning materials, and insecticides; harmful are pencil leads, ballpoint and felt-tip pens, alcohol, coffee, avocado, and strong spices.	Remove all poisonous items from the bird's environment, or prevent it from reaching them. Be particularly careful about lead curtain weights—parrots like to gnaw on them; remove weights, if this is possible. Maintain wing-feather trims and teach the bird to stay in bird-proofed areas.
Poisonous trees, bushes, houseplants	Severe disturbances, often fatal.	Don't give the bird any branches of poisonous trees or bushes to gnaw. For example, the following are poisonous: acacia, yew, laburnum, viburnum, black honeysuckle, holly, dwarf elder, and many of the needle evergreens. Keep the parrot from nibbling or eating houseplants. Maintain wing-feather trims and teach the bird to stay in bird-proofed areas.
Smoking	Contaminated air damages delicate air sacs. Nicotine can contribute to feather picking or be fatal.	Don't smoke in the vicinity of the bird. Air the rooms regularly (avoid drafts!). Cigarettes and ashtrays should be kept out of the bird's reach.
Temperature changes	Catching cold or freezing at lower temperatures, for example, if the heat goes off.	Avoid abrupt changes of temperature as much as possible; continually check the heating system; insulate the bird house.

A Rose-breasted cockatoo playing with a length of rope.

Toy time for this Leadbeater's cockatoo.

Showering (indoor cage): If the cockatoo has no bathing dish in its cage, it must be showered at least a couple of times weekly so that it can get rid of its feather dust. Smaller cages—without the droppings tray—may be placed, bird and all, in the bathtub and showered with a gentle spray of lukewarm water. Recently acquired birds should become accustomed to the shower slowly. Leave the cage in its usual place and carefully spray the cockatoo through the cage bars with a clean spray bottle that has never contained insecticides. In time the cockatoo will become so comfortable with this procedure that it will make happy sounds and spread its wings in anticipation at the mere sight of the spray bottle. Shower in the morning hours; this will permit the plumage to dry again by evening.

Claw Trimming: Cockatoos that are mostly kept in a cage can develop overgrown claws, despite perches with rough surfaces. The bird will have difficulty grasping, and the claws must be trimmed. To do this, take the parrot in your hand, grasp its toes between two fingers, and cut the claws with a sharp nail trimmer. Many cockatoos can be taught to submit to nail grooming without being wrapped in a towel, as veterinarians do, some will not. In addition you should smooth the cut sur-faces with a nail file. Avoid the blood vessel, which extends down into the claws. In the dark cockatoo claws, the blood vessels are hard to see. For this reason, you should have expert claw cutting demonstrated by a veterinarian or professional groomer prior to your first time doing it!

Beak Trimming: Overgrowth of the horn of the beak can occur if the cockatoo doesn't have enough gnawing material available (see page 19). A metabolic disturbance resulting from an unbalanced diet can also lead to malformation of the beak, which will hinder the cockatoo's ability to eat. Only an experienced avian veterinarian or groomer should undertake beak correction.

Wing-feather Trimming: Trimming wing feathers is absolutely necessary for a cockatoo who is allowed much liberty in the home. If the bird keeps leaving its perch, it is in danger of having a number of household accidents, including drowning, being burned on a stovetop, electrocution, smashing into ceiling fans, and poisoning (see Table of Dangers, page 29). Never trim the long flight feathers too short to easily regrow, that is, shorter than the coverts (feathers that

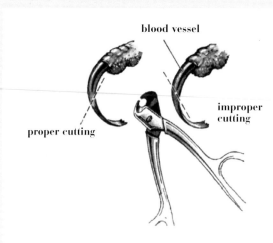

blood vessel

proper cutting

improper cutting

Cutting claws: Left, correctly done; right, incorrectly done. Be very careful not to injure the blood vessel!

cover the base of the primaries). Never trim more than eight to ten flight feathers, counting from the outside. For most cockatoos, trimming about one half to two thirds of the length of five or six flight feathers is sufficient to safely ground them indoors. No wing trim should be trusted outdoors. Cockatoos should go outdoors only within the protection of a cage or carrier.

Cleaning the Cage and Aviary

Daily: Rinse out feed and water dishes with hot water, dry, and refill. Remove debris around the cage with the vacuum cleaner; wipe away dust, because cockatoos shed feather dust.

Weekly: Empty droppings tray twice weekly and change newspaper.

Monthly: Thoroughly scrub the cage, droppings tray, and all the appropriate items in the cage under hot water and then dry. If you use a disinfectant, make sure it's one that is expressly for use with cage birds, possibly available through your pet dealer or veterinarian. Follow directions exactly! For some of the disinfectants, gloves are recommended. Be sure to rinse the parrot cage thoroughly and dry out well before returning the cockatoo. Watch for strong odors; they can be toxic.

Care of Aviary Birds

In contrast to the care measures of house birds, cockatoos that live in outdoor aviaries with a bird shelter need few maneuvers. Beak and claw trimming are not required as a rule, because the parrots usually have the opportunity to grind down claws and beak on the rough branches of different sizes. Beak growth is regulated naturally by gnawing natural wooden branches and nest boxes.

Proper wing clipping: Trim the secondaries and the inner primaries (the white part) on both wings. Remember, never clip just one wing—the cockatoo would lose its balance when trying to take off.

Showering (outdoor aviary): Although cockatoos in the outdoor aviary can bathe in a rain shower or a bath that is placed at their disposal, installation of a sprinkler system is recommended for larger aviaries. During warm summer months the system is turned on daily for a short time around midday. The plumage of the cockatoos will dry again by evening.

Small Wounds: In flight, a cockatoo often bangs against the fencing of the flight cage and so injures the sensitive skin of the nose. Also, bites on the toes acquired in fighting with rivals are not infrequent. Although sometimes such wounds bleed a great deal, it usually isn't necessary to call in the veterinarian. Rather, leave the injured bird completely at rest to give the bleeding a chance to stop. If this does not happen within a few minutes, however, apply Stay (Mardel Laboratories, Inc.) immediately as birds have a small total blood volume. Excessive blood loss can lead quickly to stress, weakness, breathing difficulties, unconsciousness, and death.

DIET

The diet of free cockatoos is quite varied, depending on their habitat. Some cockatoo species have developed specialized diets. Those that live in the grasslands of interior Australia mainly eat small seeds, including wheat field kernels found in cultivated areas.

Cockatoos that live in the tropical rainforests are not specialized feeders, for they find quite a varied diet in their natural habitat at all seasons of the year.

Manufactured Diets

Although cockatoos in the wild can consume all manner of seed, seed is no longer considered a good basic diet for indoor cockatoos. Companion cockatoos, which can live for decades, don't fly, or forage, or find and defend nest sites. All these wild activities stimulate the bird's physique, while a companion parrot may not have nearly so many opportunities for exercise.

A companion cockatoo can easily become obese and malnourished on a mostly-seed diet. Modern parrot diets are the product of years of scientific research and are designed with the long-lived cage bird in mind. Each bite the bird eats contains appropriately balanced nutrients while also providing necessary vitamins and minerals. My favorites are Harrison's (an

A healthy diet for your cockatoo is very important. Here, a Sulfur-crested cockatoo enjoys a citrus treat.

organic bird diet) and Roudybush, but there are many good diets on the market. Read the labels. Look for lots of real-food ingredients rather than added chemicals.

While most modern parrot diets claim to be "complete nutrition," it is probably best to offer at least one third of the diet in other foods.

Fruit, Green Feed, Sprouted Feed

Fruit and Vegetables: Fruits, vegetables, sprouted seeds, and cooked pasta contain important vitamins and minerals. After becoming acclimated, parrots will eat all fruits and vegetables that the store or your garden has to offer: apples, pears, plums, peaches, pomegranates, raisins, cherries, grapes, but they also do not reject exotic fruits such as oranges, bananas, mangos, papayas, or kiwis. Be sure to remove pits from apples, plums, and peaches as these can be poisonous. In addition, berry fruits of all kinds (strawberries, cranberries, blueberries, gooseberries, or red currants and mountain ash berries) as well as rose hips, are acceptable. Among the vegetables and greens, they like carrots and carrot tops, cucumbers, spinach, broccoli, celery, cooked sweet potatoes, pea pods, pumpkin, and zucchini.

Note: The fresh corn kernels full of milk that are available in the fall may be given occasionally, but corn itself is so tasty and has so little nutritional value that it should

During feeding, the cockatoo uses its foot to hold onto larger pieces of food.

Producing Sprouted Feed: Place a two-days' supply of seeds in a dish, cover them with water, and let the seed kernels soak in a warm place for 24 hours. Then shake the swollen seeds in a fine-meshed sieve while rinsing thoroughly. Now spread the seeds out on a flat screen. Put them in a warm place again. During the next 24 hours, rinse the seeds thoroughly under running water several times. Depending upon the degree of warmth, the seeds will have sprouted after two or three days. They should be rinsed once more and given to the cockatoos in a separate feeding dish. Give the birds only as much as they can eat within a few hours.

Caution: Sprouted feed spoils quickly, so you must remove the leftovers within a few hours, especially in summer, and clean the dish.

Hard-shelled and tree nuts such as almonds, hazel nuts, pecans, and Brazil nuts may be given, but only as treats. Avoid peanuts, as they grow in the ground and can spread diseases, molds, and fungi.

be given only as treats. The palette of suitable green feeds ranges from garden vegetables (spinach, lettuce, or chard) to countless wild plants, such as shepherd's purse, chickweed, and dandelion. Wash all fruits and vegetables thoroughly before feeding them; they may have been sprayed with insecticides.

Sprouted Feed: In winter, when fruits and vegetables are expensive, sprouted feed can fulfill the cockatoos' vitamin and mineral requirements. Appropriate seeds are oats, wheat, and sprouted or soaked small seeds, such as those sold for parakeets. Each type of seed is sprouted separately and then combined in one dish at feeding time.

Animal Protein

Although cockatoos are primarily plant-eaters, their bodies also need regular supplies of protein in small amounts. Most modern parrot diets are formulated to provide this and are not intended to be supplemented with animal protein. However, an occasional piece of a thoroughly hard-boiled egg, a little tofu, tuna, or low-fat mozzarella cheese may be offered weekly as a treat.

TIP

Trained Owners?

It is especially important to purchase a fully weaned bird, more so for new owners of cockatoos than for any other type of parrot. Cockatoos are said to be very emotionally dependent, very codependent, and very manipulative. Its not unusual for severe behavioral problems to develop in cockatoos that were purchased unweaned. For example, breeders and parrot behavior consultants often report being asked to help finish weaning cockatoos that are well past one year old.

In one case, the Moluccan cockatoo was two years old and would not eat anything except food from a human hand when in the care of the humans who attempted to wean it. In another case, also a Moluccan cockatoo, the bird would eat nothing except green peas, provided one at a time from the hand of the caregiver.

Both of these cases proved behavioral in origin and were related to the birds' relationships with their owners. The birds had trained the humans.

In both cases, when the birds were moved to a different home where there were different humans and other fully-weaned cockatoos, they were quite willing to eat independently. When they were in the homes of the novice owners who tried to wean them, both birds screamed incessantly and refused to eat anything provided in a bowl. It was a battle of wills that the birds always won. When the birds were placed in a cockatoo-specific culture with humans who had different relationships with them, these charming pink giants immediately adopted the behavior of the culture.

Inappropriate Food

Human food, such as sausage, highly seasoned meat, french fries, or gumdrops, is not parrot food and can be very harmful to the bird. Fruit pits, including apple, can be toxic, as are avocado, caffeine, and chocolate.

Rearing Feed

During the brooding period and the raising of the young, the cockatoos should be fed the breeding or high-performance formula of your favorite diet. Supplementary soft foods can be given. Grind up your regular parrot diet in the blender as a basis and enrich it with grated fruit, carrots, cottage cheese, feed calcium, and vitamins. Mix them all carefully until the feed has a damp, crumbly consistency.

The rearing feed should be offered to the cockatoos in a separate feeding bowl. It's possible that the parrots will accept this strange feed only after being offered it several times. Adjustment to the food already should have taken place by the time the young hatch so that there will be no interruption in feeding while the young are being raised.

A close-up of the Umbrella cockatoo's magnificent plumage.

A Citron cockatoo stretches its wings.

Vitamins and Minerals

Vitamin preparations are unneccessary with a good-quality, modern, scientifically formulated diet. Actually, supplementing some vitamins may even be harmful. If you suspect that your bird needs vitamin or mineral supplementation, this should be determined only by an experienced avian veterinarian. For more information on important vitamins, see the table on page 43.

Drinking Water

Cockatoos need fresh tap water daily. In areas where the water quality is poor, the drinking water should be filtered or bottled water should be used. On warm summer days, change the drinking water twice or three times daily.

Correct Feeding

Number of Feeding Dishes: There should be at least three feeding dishes available: one will hold the basic diet, another drinking water, the third fruits, vegetables, or sprouted feed in rotation. At brooding another dish is needed for rearing feed.

Note: Make sure that the dishes are always clean and that the cockatoos receive the same dishes in the usual order!

Feeding Time: Always feed at the same time, twice daily, in the morning and afternoon. Give only as much food as can be consumed in an hour and remove all but a few dry chunks of the basic diet, leaving them for a snack later.

Makeup of the Feed: The offered feed should consist of two thirds basic diet and one third fresh foods. Before and during the raising of young, the portion of the sprouted feed can be increased and the usual feed portion increased by the addition of rearing feed and cooked legumes (see Cockatoo Breeding, page 53).

Quantities: The size of the daily portion varies according to the size and the mobility of the cockatoos. For example, cage birds who have little opportunity for exercise need less food than larger cockatoo species and birds that live in aviaries. Don't skimp on the amount of feed, but also be careful not to overfeed.

Cleanliness and Hygiene

To prevent the spread of disease, it's important that all utensils used in feeding your cockatoo be kept very clean. They should be cleaned daily, and the empty seed hulls should be removed from the rest of the seed before refilling the containers. Many beginners make the mistake of putting fresh seed right on top of the old, hulls and all. This can lead to the lower seed never being used and becoming old, serving as a perfect breeding ground for bacteria and pests. Also, be sure not to introduce moist seeds to the feeder—these can become moldy and endanger the bird's health.

Food vessels and water containers from cages and aviaries should be also be cleaned regularly. A solution of household bleach and water makes a good disinfectant.

Fat-soluble Vitamins

Vitamin	Functions	Good Sources
A	Maintenance of skin, bones, and mucous membranes; prevention of night blindness; metabolism of body cells	Egg yolk; leafy greens; yellow and orange vegetables
D3	Essential for blood clotting; prevents egg binding; promotes absorption of calcium	Fish liver oils and egg yolk
E	Important for development of brain cells, muscles, blood, sex organs, and the embryo; increases blood circulation	Wheat germ; fruits and vegetables; chickweed; spinach; germinated seeds
K	Promotes blood clotting and liver functions	Green food; carrot tops; alfalfa; tomatoes; egg yolk; soy oil

Water-soluble Vitamins

Vitamin	Functions	Good Sources
B1 (Thiamin)	Assists in overall growth and metabolic functions; growth of muscles and nervous system	Yeast; fruit; eggs; liver; legumes
B2 (Riboflavin)	Development of skin, feathers, beak, and nails; egg production; metabolic functions	Eggs; green leaves; yeast; germ of good quality seeds
B3 (Niacin)	Proper function of nervous and digestive systems; hormone production	Peanuts; whole grains; corn; liver; lean meats
B6 (Pyridoxine)	Production of digestive juices, red blood cells, and antibodies	Bananas; peanuts; beans; whole grain cereal; egg yolk
B12 (Cyanocobalamin)	Essential for metabolism; assists production of red blood cells	Liver; insects; fish meal; eggs
C (Ascorbic acid)	Tissue growth; healing of wounds; red blood cell formation; promotes iron absorption	Citrus fruits and juices; leafy greens; fresh fruits; cabbage

HEALTH AND ILLNESS

Properly maintained and cared-for cockatoos seldom become ill. But even an experienced parrot keeper can make a maintenance mistake once in a while, or the cockatoo's natural resistance might be weakened for some unknown reason so that it succumbs to illness. There are no specific signs of illness for most parrot ailments, but nevertheless it is apparent when a cockatoo feels sick (see Choosing a Healthy Cockatoo, page 13).

First-aid Measures

Only an experienced avian veterinarian who has taken blood and fecal samples and tested them is in a position to evaluate whether a parrot's illness is of a serious or mild nature. Novice parrot keepers should always consult an avian veterinarian promptly upon purchase of a new bird or at the first sign of illness. A sick cockatoo must be separated immediately from other parrots and removed to an individual cage (quarantine cages offered by pet dealers are excellent).

The Visit to the Avian Veterinarian

If the condition of the cockatoo does not improve within a day, a trip to the veterinarian

The exotic Black Palm cockatoo.

is unavoidable. Find out at the time you get your cockatoo which veterinarians have the required experience in treating parrots. Keep the bird warm and quiet until it is taken to the avian veterinarian.

Transporting the bird must be done with as much protection for the bird as possible. This can best be accomplished by using a rigid plastic and metal carrier such as those sold for cats and dogs.

The doctor's questions about maintenance conditions, the bird's behavior, and the signs of illness should be answered precisely. This will make the diagnosis substantially easier.

A fecal sample from the bird is sometimes very helpful for a precise diagnosis. It probably should be examined at the outset.

The veterinarian will draw blood and send it away for testing to determine things such as the bird's white blood cell count and the condition of various internal organs. Unless the veterinarian is sure of what's wrong based on other evidence, such as the history of other companion birds in your care, don't allow antibiotic treatment until after the tests have returned. Some supportive treatments such as rehydrating with subcutaneous fluids, but not antibiotic therapy, may be done immediately.

Successful healing is usually achieved only if you follow the veterinarian's instructions exactly. For instance, stopping the treatment too early can lead to relapse.

Common Illnesses

Infestation with Endoparasites (Internal Parasites)

Parrots are mainly attacked by tapeworms (Cestoda), roundworms (Ascaridia), and threadworms (Capillaria).

Symptoms: The ailing bird sits around, often with ruffled feathers, slowly wastes away, and deposits slimy feces. Sudden death can occur as a result of intestinal obstruction by hundreds of worms (usually roundworms).

Possible Causes: Dirty maintenance conditions promote the illness.

Immediate Measures: Fecal examination at the appearance of the first sign of illness (proper treatment can lessen the extent and the consequences of the worm infestation).

Treatment: By the veterinarian, who is the only one who can prescribe appropriate medication. Follow the dosage instructions exactly. An overdose can be dangerous for the parrot.

Prevention: Regularly clean the bird cages and houses thoroughly. The droppings of parrots that live in an outdoor cage should be examined several times a year for worms.

Intestinal Inflammation

Symptoms: General signs of illness (see page 45), diarrhea, increased water intake (as a result of high fluid loss), diminished food intake, so that this illness can sometimes mean a serious threat to the life of the parrot.

Note: Psychological factors can lead to loose droppings, which should not be considered the result of an intestinal inflammation. For example, the sight of a predatory bird flying in the air or of a cat lurking on the roof of the aviary, anxiety at being caught by the keeper, or an encounter with a rival bird can lead to sudden, watery droppings.

Possible Causes: Spoiled feed, change of diet, intake of poisonous material (for example, lead, lead weights in curtains, plastic ties like those for bread bags, varnish, cleaning materials), colds, bacterial infections, e.g., Coccidiosis, *E. Coli*, and Salmonella), fungi, viruses, parasites, tumors, diseases of other organs, and practically any type of medication.

Immediate Measures: If you suspect poisoning (especially by lead!), take a fecal sample and go to the veterinarian as quickly as possible. Otherwise offer chamomile tea, some easily digested food, and keep the bird warmer than usual.

Treatment: The veterinarian must order a course of medication. Follow instructions exactly!

Prevention: Avoid causes or constantly check maintenance.

Respiratory Ailments

Dysfunctions of the respiratory organs can result from very different causes. A diagnosis is exceedingly important but is sometimes impossible in a living bird.

Symptoms: General signs of illness (see page 45), repeated sneezing, damp or stuffed-up nostrils, discharge from the nose, labored breathing (the bird sits with legs spread, breathes with open beak, and the tail moves conspicuously up and down with every breath), noisy breathing; occasionally conjunctivitis of the eyelid also occurs.

Possible Causes: Attack on the respiratory passages by bacteria, virus, or fungus.

Immediate Measures: Keep the bird warm. If there is no improvement after 12 hours, the

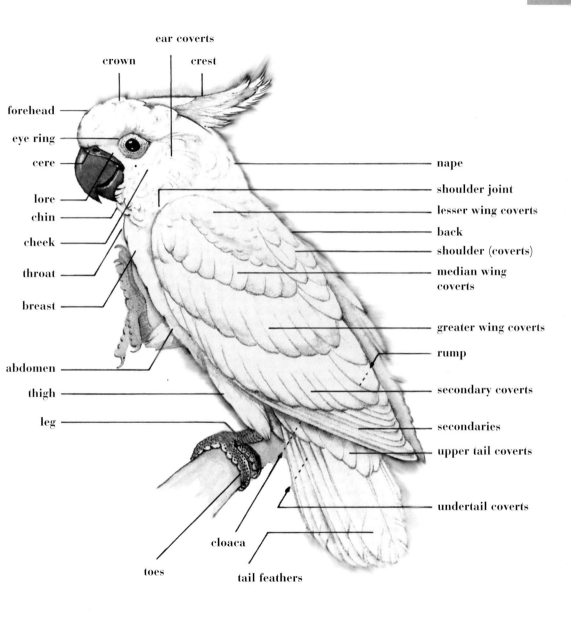

ear coverts

crown   crest

forehead

eye ring

cere

lore

chin

cheek

throat

breast

abdomen

thigh

leg

toes

cloaca

tail feathers

nape

shoulder joint

lesser wing coverts

back

shoulder (coverts)

median wing coverts

greater wing coverts

rump

secondary coverts

secondaries

upper tail coverts

undertail coverts

Names of body parts of the cockatoo can be useful to know, especially if you need to visit the veterinarian.

A Long-billed Corella cockatoo.

A pair of Moluccan cockatoos.

parrot needs a veterinarian's help. With serious breathing difficulty or noisy breathing, get to the avian veterinarian at once!

Treatment: Only by an avian veterinarian. Starting treatment promptly can increase the chance of cure. New treatments available in the last decade offer amazing potential.

Feather Eating, Feather Plucking

An uncommon manifestation that may belong more in the behavioral illnesses category. It can occur in parrots kept singly or in pairs and can occur in optimal maintenance conditions.

Symptoms: Ranges from constant pulling out and chewing of single feathers, especially in the shoulder, inner wing, breast, and legs, to the complete stripping of the body (with the exception of the unreachable head feathers). Cases of self-mutilation, even to the extent that the skin or the underlying musculature are gnawed, have also been reported.

Possible Causes: Nicotine poisoning, staph infections of the skin, or any disease causing stress to the bird can trigger feather plucking. Allergies are sometimes suspected (avoid peanuts). Usually several of the following factors are present when this vice appears:
✔ insufficient exercise; cage too small
✔ boredom in sterile accommodations
✔ prolonged stress in overcrowded conditions in a cage or aviary
✔ lack of sleep
✔ lack of or loss of a favorite person
✔ lack of a mate at the beginning of sexual maturity
✔ skin ailment that causes itching, or heavy molt
✔ inadequate diet, wrong temperature in the environment, insufficient humidity
✔ lack of opportunity for bathing or lack of regular showering

Treatment: Avoid faulty care and maintenance! Frequently remove the feathers that fall to the bottom of the cage. In some cases it is advisable to transfer the affected parrot from a cage to a larger aviary complete with extensive opportunities for exercise in the form of gnawing branches, chains, wooden toys, rope ends, or climbing apparatus; if necessary put the bird with a companion bird. Pay attention to your single bird more often and more intensively! Allow the bird 10 to 12 hours of sleep in a darkened room. Consult an avian veterinarian,

Feather plucking: Cockatoos that pull out their feathers to the point of almost complete baldness usually have psychological ailments.

and then if health issues are eliminated, an experienced parrot behavior consultant.

Prevention: Optimal living conditions. Behavioral therapy emphasizing independence and curiosity.

Parrot Fever (Psittacosis)

Parrot fever or psittacosis is by no means a common illness of parrots. Nevertheless, it should be discussed briefly because the name is very familiar to lay people and it can produce serious and to some degree life-threatening symptoms in parrots and humans. Psittacosis is an infectious illness which is not limited to parrots. The microorganism that causes this disease has been identified in more than a hundred other bird species (the term *ornithosis* is used in these cases).

Symptoms: No characteristic symptoms. Sleepiness, weight loss, diarrhea, inflammation of eye membranes, and diminished food intake can be concomitant signs of the illness.

Treatment: Under the care of an avian veterinarian with an appropriate antibiotic.

Note: For humans, a psittacosis infection can become a life-threatening illness. Besides moderate symptoms, similar to those of a cold or flu, severe illness with high fever and infection of the lungs also has been observed. The disease is curable if it is recognized and treated in time.

Prevention: Scarcely possible; it is important that the parrot be acquired disease-free. Be careful about buying parrots kept in crowded cages and under unhygienic conditions.

Psittacine Beak and Feather Disease (PBFD)

Since about 1980, a plumage disease (Psittacine Beak and Feather Disease or PBFD) has appeared. This disease is considered uncommon in parrots, but it appeared first in cockatoos and is more common in cockatoos than in other parrots.

Symptoms: Affected cockatoos will first lose powder down on the feathers, then new feathers begin coming in clubbed or rounded rather than pointed and do not mature properly. In its beginning stages this illness may resemble feather plucking, the plumage becomes increasingly full of holes, until finally the growth of feathers comes to a halt. The cockatoo is unable to fly. In addition, a softening of the beak can be observed in some cases. The bird's immune system will be compromised, and some birds infected with PBFD die from this cause, with the cofactor of whatever disease the bird ultimately succumbs to. Some young birds die quickly without ever showing symptoms of PBFD.

Possible Causes: This disease is caused by a virus that is primarily transmitted in the nest box or during handfeeding. PBFD can be diagnosed with a blood test, but a positive blood test does not mean the bird will die of the disease or even exhibit symptoms of the disease. It should be presumed that a bird with a positive test for PBFD is contagious, however, and the bird should be quarantined until the bird is retested and shows negative for PBFD.

Treatment: If the bird is not showing symptoms, but shows a positive test for PBFD, all efforts should be made to boost the bird's immune system and protect the bird from other diseases. An avian veterinarian can treat specific complaints caused by immune system failure and make the bird more comfortable, but there is no cure, as yet, for PBFD.

Prevention: Avoid contact with infected birds. Wash hands and change clothing after visiting unfamiliar parrots, such as birds for sale.

COCKATOO BREEDING

Greater and Lesser Sulphur-crested and Rose-breasted cockatoos breed in human captivity the best of all the large parrot species—provided they have the right living conditions. To be successful with breeding, you must provide some basic requirements (especially in living arrangements and diet).

Species Protection

Cockatoos are among the species of animals that are endangered or threatened with extinction. The cause of this is the ongoing destruction of their habitat. Expanses of forest are being recklessly destroyed in order to gain usable land area, and with them the breeding and sleeping trees of many cockatoo species are falling victim to the power saw. Successful conservation can be achieved only with the combination of species protection by law and purposeful cockatoo breeding by zoos and fanciers.

Species Overpopulation

Curiously, even though several cockatoo species are threatened in the wild, the same species may be considered "overpopulated" in captivity. Because cockatoos can live for a

Watch your beard around this Goffin named "Spooky"!

very long time and because their needs are very great, there appear to be more cockatoos in captivity than there are homes capable of accommodating them over the long term. Rescue organizations and shelters, especially in affluent areas, report that their own facilities are becoming increasingly crowded with cockatoos.

Before beginning a cockatoo breeding program, talk to bird clubs, retailers, and breeders familiar with the species you wish to breed to ensure that you are making a wise decision, both ethically and financially. Existing breeders can contribute to the protection of the species by donating fertile eggs for introduction into wild nests. In this way, cockatoos of common species in the wild can learn to incubate and raise baby cockatoos of rarer species to successfully live in the wild.

Prerequisites for Successful Breeding

Housing: Housing a cockatoo pair in a bird room or in an outdoor aviary, rather than a high-traffic family room, offers the best conditions for successful breeding. Pairs should be somewhat removed from family comings and goings or traffic noise. If you have a system of several aviaries together, you should make sure that the breeding pair isn't disturbed by neighbor birds during its courtship preparations (erect screens if necessary).

Additions to the Diet During Breeding: If you feed your cockatoos a balanced, varied diet, nutrient supplements before and during breeding are unnecessary as a rule. Nevertheless, it's a good idea to maintain a certain seasonal rhythm in the composition of the feed for birds you plan to use for breeding. Try to give the birds a sense of harvest time, for wild birds reproduce in a cycle designed to feed babies when food supplies are greatest.

Nest Boxes: The nest box should have a square base (see drawing below) and can be obtained from the pet store or can be made at home if you are handy with tools. Reinforce the edges of the entry hole with strips of tin, to prevent the cockatoos from expanding the entry hole with their beaks. Underneath the entrance hole (inside the box) fasten strong, wide-meshed rectangular wire fencing to serve as a climbing aid.

Litter for the Nest Box: Equip nest boxes or hollow trees with a layer of wood humus about 4 inches (10 cm) thick, which should be slightly dampened shortly before the time of nesting. This way the eggs will settle properly under the weight of the female.

Mounting Nest Boxes: Nesting places are attached high under the roof of the aviary (in a garden aviary, in the roofed-over part) or in the bird shelter under the roof. If possible, place them so that you can easily examine the brooding hole or nest box without startling the birds.

Note: Cockatoos nest only at the time of brooding. After brooding, the hollow trees and nest boxes must be thoroughly cleaned, disinfected, repaired if necessary, and stored dry until the next reproduction period.

Pairing

Even if you have a known male and a known female (see Determining Gender, page 14), it's not easy to establish a harmonious pair. All birds intended for breeding should belong to the same species or subspecies. Grown birds can become used to each other with difficulty (see Getting Used to Each Other, page 27). On the other hand, if several young birds of different genders live together in one aviary, harmonious cockatoo pair bonds usually develop quickly and spontaneously.

Sometimes spontaneous pairing also occurs in adult birds as it does with young birds. It also can happen, however, that two cockatoos will not adjust to each other, even after several attempts. In this case the bird must be exchanged as soon as possible.

Suitable brooding holes. Left, a hollowed-out tree trunk (available in pet stores) with a removable door on the side. Right, a homemade nest box with a removable roof.

During mating, the female lies flat on the perch with wings folded, indicating her receptiveness to copulation.

Brooding Period

With cockatoos that are kept in an indoor aviary or in a bird room, the brooding period can occur at any season. If the parrots live in an outdoor aviary and winter over in the bird shelter, the brooding birds eventually establish a seasonal rhythm. Brooding season begins about the end of April (egg laying at the beginning of May, hatching of young at the beginning of June, and young leaving the nest from the middle of July to the beginning of August, with stragglers somewhat later). Molting occurs in September and October. After that the cockatoos go into a winter rest period until the next spring.

Courtship and Mating

In many cockatoo species the courtship behavior is very impressive.

Display Behavior: With spread feathers and wings, fanned tail, and erect crest feathers, the male woos the female. This so called display behavior serves on one hand to scare off rival suitors, on the other to court the female.

Mutual Preening: Another courtship behavior often seen is mutual preening (see drawing, page 6), the mutual "scratching" of two birds. This behavior has a social function in that it serves to strengthen pair bonding. Both birds can enjoy preening on places like the head or rump area that a single bird can reach only with difficulty by itself.

Copulation: Courtship usually leads to mating. The male mounts the female so that their cloacas (into which both the spermatic duct and the oviduct empty) are joined and so copulation is accomplished. Shortly before egg laying, the readiness to mate and the frequency of copulation increases.

Egg Laying and Brooding

The end of the courtship period is followed by egg laying. At intervals of two to three days—in the afternoon or early morning—the cockatoo female lays two to three uniformly white, round-oval eggs. In the species described here, the female and male take turns brooding, although the greater part of it falls to the female. Both parents can get food independently of each other from time to time. For this reason cockatoos lack the partner-feeding behavior noted in other parrots, a social pattern in which the male provides the female and

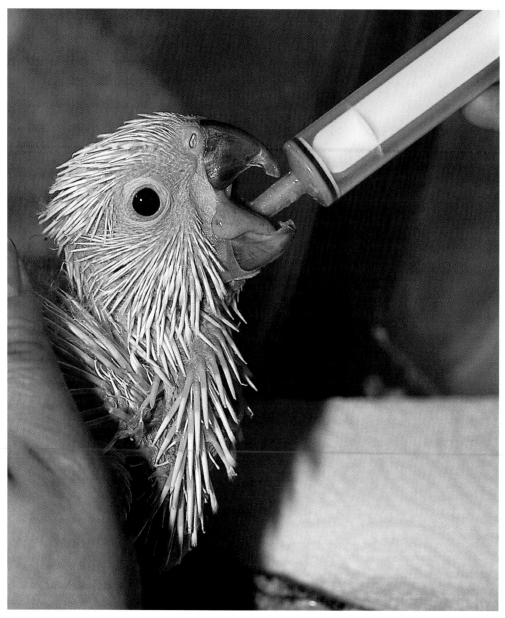

A baby Sulfur-crested getting its nutrients.

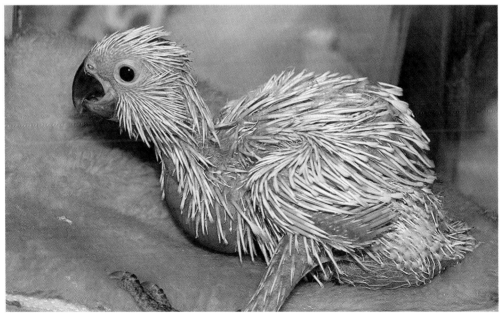

Above, Goffin cockatoos at four weeks, and below, a baby Sulfur-crested cockatoo.

The Greater Sulfur-crested cockatoo at 25 days—eyes are open, and the quills have begun to break through the skin.

pletely helpless. Their bodily development takes a fairly long time; they open their eyes only after several weeks, and a thick coat of down develops to protect them from the cold. Between 60 and 100 days—depending on the species—the young cockatoos get their complete plumage and can leave the nest. Before they are completely independent, however, they pass a further two to three weeks in which they are cared for and fed by their parents.

Note: Cockatoos as a rule raise only one young bird out of a two- or three-egg clutch. The remaining one or two eggs are a reserve, so to speak, in case something goes wrong with the oldest nestling in the first few days. But if the firstborn bird develops normally, the feeding and care of the younger animals is sometimes neglected so that they often pine away or die prematurely. In this case, the breeder can try to raise the younger birds by hand.

the young with food during the brooding and raising periods.

The length of the brooding period, depending on the species (see Frequently Kept Cockatoo Species, page 70), is somewhere between 25 and 30 days.

Development of the Young

Young cockatoos hatch at the same intervals at which the eggs were laid. At birth they are—like all altricial birds—naked, blind, and com-

Hand–raising

Hand-raising may be necessary when cockatoos leave their eggs because of frequent disturbance or because they can't give enough care to all the young. If a breeder notices this soon enough, he or she can take the eggs from the nest and continue developing them in an incubator. Young birds hatched in an incubator, or nestlings that have been neglected by their

Again at about five weeks—the quills can be seen on the head, and the beak darkens in color.

At 40 days—the yellow crest feathers are visible and a portion of the wing and back plumage has appeared.

parents, may be raised by hand.

One drawback to hand-raising is, of course, that the young birds are completely dependent on humans and sometimes cannot be used later for breeding.

Housing: Keep the parrot chicks at a temperature of about 97°F (36°C). An infrared lamp is very good for this. Choose a container for keeping the nestling that isn't too large (a hospital cage or a wooden box with a glass front). The quarters should be controlled thermostatically. The temperature should be reduced gradually as the birds mature.

Food and Feeding: At the very beginning, neonatal cockatoos should have a quality hand feeding formula, preferably the same brand you have been feeding the parents, every two hours between 6 A.M. and 12 P.M. Only fresh food should be offered at every feeding. Temperature should be 104 to 105.8°F (40–41°C) at feeding; in the beginning it can be administered with a large volume plastic eyedropper, and later with a teaspoon (the sides of which have been bent inwards). With increasing age, the young birds are fed only every three to four hours. As the birds near weaning, other foods may be added and offered lukewarm or even at room temperature.

It is difficult to manage the crossover to eating independently. Get the young cockatoos used to it step by step. At first give them the familiar formula in the feeding dish, then later soft fruit and greenery, and finally diet pellets, first broken up, then whole. Young cockatoos accomplish this most easily by watching older neighboring birds.

Be careful to see that the young birds are never subject to sudden temperature changes or drafts. Only when they are fully feathered should cockatoo young be kept at room temperature without any additional heat source.

What to Watch Out for During Brooding

Brooding is an exceptional situation for the cockatoos as well as for the breeder; therefore:

✔ If possible don't enter the aviary during the brooding period, for some cockatoos become very aggressive and will attack.

✔ Avoid disturbances, such as building alterations or large cleaning operations, and keep visitors away from the brooding birds.

✔ Before and during the raising of the young, provide a variety of fresh foods as well as manufactured diet in sufficient quantities.

✔ In especially dry summer months the nest boxes must be sprayed with water on the outside about once a day.

✔ Make sure that the brooding birds always have an opportunity to bathe.

UNDERSTANDING COCKATOOS

How Cockatoos Live Together in Nature

Quite a bit is known about the way of life and the behavior of cockatoos in their natural habitat—in contrast to most of the other parrot species.

Group Size

The cockatoo species that are described in this book live together in flocks except during the brooding period. Such flocks consist of single animals, pairs, and families that gather at common eating, drinking, and sleeping places. While searching for food, cockatoos—particularly those of the plains and desert habitats—congregate in large groups. Often one will encounter groups of several thousand birds at favorite spots. In contrast, groups of those species that are found in the tropical rain forests outside the Australian continent are much smaller, containing only eight to ten birds.

The Communal Life

Gathering into groups functions primarily to ensure that the cockatoos will find food. Meeting social needs cannot be assumed to be an important function because the birds in the group don't usually enter into any closer social

This Citron cockatoo seems pretty attached to its rattle!

bonds—except for the choice of mate. Rather, the communal life can be characterized as a kind of open association in which the individual animals don't necessarily know each other and in which there is no firmly defined order of dominance. The advantage of a federation is that feeding places can be better scouted and can be secured against rival feeders. Of course there are also frequent quarrels within the cockatoo association about the best feeding places, sleeping places, and nest holes.

Brooding Season

Among cockatoos, the urge to brood is dependent on the environmental conditions. This means that the birds will be impelled to breed when plant growth has reached its height and also when weather conditions are best. Pairs that are ready to breed separate from the group and go searching for nest holes. Rotted-out tree trunks or abandoned woodpecker holes serve as brooding holes. Usually the holes are enlarged with the cockatoo's strong beak. The shavings that fall into the hole as a result of this process are used by the cockatoos as a bed for their eggs. As a rule they don't bring in additional nest material.

The cockatoos of the tropical rain forests of the Indonesian islands set about breeding after the rainy season and try to occupy the same nest holes every year. Cockatoo species that inhabit the arid areas of the Australian interior lead a nomadic or partially nomadic life. Presumably they breed yearly—according to the food supply—in various districts. Egg laying, clutch size, and brooding time vary from species to species. After the young hatch, the parent cockatoos are busy raising them for many weeks. Afterwards the parents and their young join as a family group with other cockatoos in a close flock, which remains in existence until the next breeding season.

Expected Behavior in Companion Cockatoos

Eating and Drinking

The cockatoo removes the outer coverings from seeds, fruits, and vegetables in its beak with its tongue. Like most large parrots, the cockatoo uses its foot like a hand, to hold morsels of food and lift food to its beak. To drink, the bird scoops up water with its lower beak and tips its head back to swallow.

Resting and Sleeping

Healthy birds rest and sleep on one leg; the other leg is drawn up into the feathers. The body plumage may be fluffed slightly, the head is usually turned back and tucked into the back feathers to the base of the beak. The eyes may be either closed completely or partially.

Exercise

Cockatoos that live in captivity are in nearly constant motion all day long. In the cage they climb and do gymnastics tirelessly; in outdoor aviaries you find them almost constantly climbing, scratching, gnawing, or flying.

Besides their natural motions, with training cockatoos also are able to mimic playful movements. Cockatoos are especially famous for their dexterity. There are cockatoos that can carry things, push little toy cars, eat from a spoon, and much more.

Running and Hopping: Cockatoos, especially those of the dry plains and grasslands of interior Australia, are "good on their feet," for they find their food predominantly on the ground. Birds of these species also can be observed frequently running in the aviary or cage. The cockatoo's body is held erect as it runs with long, stiff-gaited steps. Likewise, hopping is accompanied with an erect body and crest.

Scratching: Some cockatoo species love to scratch in the dirt, on the floor, or in fabric corners, such as a sofa or overstuffed chair. This behavior has developed because they find their food mainly on the ground. The most noticeable adaptation to this form of food seeking is seen in the slender-billed cockatoo, which has an elongated upper beak suitable for digging.

Climbing: Most cockatoo species possess excellent climbing ability. Therefore you should offer your cockatoo plenty of things to climb in the cage and in the aviary.

Flying: In their natural habitat, many cockatoo species often cover long distances in their search for feeding places. They are excellent fliers. In captivity, a cockatoo must be trained and encouraged to flap a couple of times daily until it is winded. This exercise stimulates the bird's metabolism and can be a primary defense in the prevention of feather picking and excessive screaming.

Showers: Wild cockatoos sometimes fly and forage and reproduce in blinding rain.

In captivity, showering can function like exercise to help the wing-feather-trimmed birds express nervous energy that might come out as unwanted attention-demanding or feather-damaging behaviors.

Comfort Behaviors

Comfort behaviors include patterns concerned with the body care of the cockatoo.

Preening: A cockatoo preens its plumage several times daily by drawing individual feathers through its beak. The bird usually begins with the smaller feathers, then polishes the primaries and secondaries and the tail feathers. Finally, by means of rubbing movements with the head and beak, the bird distributes the feather dust over its plumage.

Head Scratching: Also as part of plumage care, the bird lifts its foot to its head and scratches while turning and twisting its head. Some cockatoos occasionally use little branches to help scratch. An unusual behavior is the hesitant, almost slow, motion head scratching that looks rather like someone swimming the crawl. This behavior is primarily seen in single birds—perhaps satisfying its need for mutual preening (see page 6) with a partner bird in this way.

Beak Care: The cockatoo removes dirt and food particles from its beak by rubbing it on a hard surface, such as the perch. Cockatoos also grind their beaks, sometimes quite noisily, as they fall asleep. Beak grinding is an absolutely normal and frequently observed comfort behavior.

This cockatoo uses a short branch to help scratch. The use of tools in performing tasks is a sign of cockatoos' intelligence.

Showering: All cockatoos love to take shower baths when they get used to the procedure. They spread their wings slightly and fan their tails. During the shower they twist and turn their whole body and flap their wings so that the feathers get damp all over.

Stretching: Stretching movements, often accompanied by yawns, frequently are observable after rest periods. The wing and leg on the same side of the body will be stretched to the rear/down, while at the same time the corresponding side of the tail will be spread. Sometimes you will also see the bird lifting both wings over its back and spreading them. Yawning stretches the beak parts, though this serves primarily to supply the body with oxygen.

Social Behavior

Even before the onset of sexual maturity the cockatoo develops social contacts, which in time lead to pair bonding.

A flock of Rose-breasted cockatoos in the wild.

Courtship Behavior

The behavior patterns of courtship serve to promote the formation of a cockatoo pair and the strengthening of this bond. The courtship behavior of young and inexperienced cockatoos is especially striking.

Display Behavior: Display behavior (see Courtship and Mating, page 55) is a kind of forerunner of true courtship. The male shows off his body to the chosen female. The male makes himself noticeable with spread tail, opened wings, ruffled feathers, and sometimes erected facial fan, ear coverts, and crest, whose colors also serve as a warning signal to rivals. The display is accompanied by choppy, angular movements, and a backward lifting and sinking of the body on the perch. This striking behavior—besides wooing the female—is intended to frighten rival males and keep them away from the female. Display therefore serves partly as threatening behavior. At first the female

The stages of the Lesser Sulfur-crested cockatoo cleaning its feathers (preening)— first the leg plumage (top left), and then the wings (upper right and bottom left). Finally, it fluffs up its plumage and shakes itself vigorously.

repulses the male's attempts to approach and avoids mating. In time however she permits the male in her vicinity.

Mutual Preening: During the courtship period the mutual scratching that is termed mutual preening has a calming, aggression-checking function. It allows the birds to get used to increasingly intensive contact, until finally copulation occurs.

Copulation: During copulation, the male mounts the female, and they mate through the joining of the cloaca, an all-purpose opening through which droppings, seminal fluids, and, eventually, eggs are passed. Between adult mates that already have several successful broods, the preliminary courtship may be shortened greatly, and in some instances spon-taneous copulation may occur. Often the female invites her partner to mate.

Threatening Behavior: Threatening behavior is very similar to display behavior. In general, threat and aggression toward presumed enemies or rivals increases with growing breeding urge. Snapping the beak and lateral presentation (forebody lowered, tail lifted, and tail feathers spread) also express an aggressive mood.

Managing Behavior in Companion Cockatoos

Young cockatoos come with great cooperation skills; therefore, step-up practice and peek-a-boos in the towel need be performed only minimally (a minute or two a couple of times a week) in order to teach and maintain cooperation skills. On the other hand, hand-fed domestic cockatoos may fail to develop emotional and behavioral independence.

Special care must be taken from the newly-weaned baby's first days in the home to encourage the development of curiosity and independent play. The bird should not be let near anything (except humans) that holds sentimental value for you—he might rip, shred, chew, or otherwise dismantle to his heart's content. The bird should be provided with many different toys of many different types and textures. Humans must also set a good example for the bird to follow by demonstrating independent activities such as knitting, typing, washing dishes, or simply reading.

Threatening behavior. Similar to courtship behavior, the cockatoo "displays" with erected crest feathers, spread wings, and fanned tail—signaling readiness for attack.

Step-up Practice

From its first days in the home, a well-socialized, newly-weaned baby cockatoo will expect lots of cuddling. The juvenile bird also needs to learn more than cuddling. A young cockatoo learns (or rather, is conditioned) to cooperate in social settings when it engages in interactive activities with people. Step-up practice is the most common of these exercises. The routine, when practiced almost daily, needs to be no more than a few minutes in duration. This interactive practice works best when it includes

1. practice stepping the bird from the hand to and from an unfamiliar perch,

2. practice stepping the bird from hand to hand,

3. practice stepping the bird from a hand-held perch to and from an unfamiliar perch,

4. practice stepping the bird from a hand-held perch to a hand-held perch, and

5. practice stepping the bird from a familiar perch to and from both hands and to and from hand-held perches.

Unless the bird is cooperative and well-patterned enough to step up from an unfamiliar perch in unfamiliar territory, it may refuse to step up from the cage or other familiar perch. In an older or unsocialized cockatoo, step-up practice might initially have to take place outside the bird's established territory in the home. A laundry room or hallway is usually perfect, as the bird will probably never spend much time in these areas, and therefore should not develop territorial behavior in them. A cooperative bird can be successfully patterned to this exercise anywhere.

Be sure to offer affection and praise after each completed step-up. Always discontinue step-up practice only after a successful completion of the command. This is crucial to good patterning. If the command is unsuccessful, alter technique, approach, or prompting mannerisms rather than continue with unsuccessful methods. Be careful not to reinforce unsuccessful patterns. Even if the bird must be placed on the floor to achieve a successful step-up command, unless the bird is having a panic reaction, don't return it to its territory until just after a successful cooperative interaction.

There is no substitute for warm, genuine human enthusiasm as a reward for the bird's success in stepping up. Especially with shy or cautious cockatoos, the most important part of this exercise is the bird's enjoyment of the process. If the bird is not eagerly cooperating with step-ups and step-up practice, something is going wrong, and an experienced parrot behavior consultant should be called in as quickly as possible.

While a young cockatoo has a need to be cuddled and snuggled, constant snuggling can become addictive to the bird, who may wish to do absolutely nothing except cuddle and preen. This can lead to over-preening, a precurser of feather chewing behaviors. It can certainly also lead to attention-demanding screaming and other attention-demanding behaviors.

COCKATOO SPECIES

Interesting Facts About Cockatoos

Parrots constitute some 320 to 330 of the approximately 8,600 bird species on the earth. In the order of parrots there are 18 cockatoo species, including the cockatiels.

Like the majority of parrots, cockatoos have a powerful, mobile curved beak and a zygodactly toe formation (four toes, two front opposing two back). Their mostly white or dark plumage, their expressive facial fans, and their long, movable forehead and crown feathers (recumbent and recurve) distinguish them visually from the other parrots.

Distribution: Cockatoos are distributed over wide areas of Australia and Indonesia. The Philippine cockatoo has the northernmost distribution area. It inhabits the Philippine island of Luzon (north latitude). The Funereal cockatoo and the Greater Sulphur-crested cockatoo have the southernmost ranges. Both species, along with others, are found on Tasmania. Cockatoos inhabit three environments: tropical rain forests with high temperatures and heavy rainfall; grassy plains as transition zones between rain forests and desert (humid and dry savannahs); and wastes with prairie-like vegetation and scant, irregular rainfall.

Cockatoo Species: The species described in this book are indicated with an asterisk.

Another Rose-breasted cockatoo.

Family: *Cacatuidae*—cockatoos
Subfamily: *Cacatuinae*—true cockatoos
Genus: *Probosciger*
Species: Palm cockatoo (*P. aterrimus*, five subspecies)
Genus: *Calyptoihynchus*
Species: Red-tailed black or Banksian cockatoo (*C. magnificus*, four subspecies)
Glossy black cockatoo (*C. lathami*)
Funereal or Yellow-tailed black cockatoo (*C. funereus*, three subspecies)
White-tailed black or Baudin's black cockatoo (*C. baudinii*, four subspecies)
Genus: *Callocephalon*
Species: Gang-gang or red-crowned or helmeted cockatoo (*C. fimbriatum*)
Genus: *Eolophus*
Species: Rose-breasted or Roseate cockatoo, galah* (*E. roseicapillus*, three subspecies)
Genus: *Cacatua*
Species: Philippine or red-vented cockatoo* (*C. haematuropygia*)
Goffin's cockatoo* (*C. goffini*)
Bare-eyed cockatoo or Little Corella (*C. sanguinea*, two subspecies)
Slender-billed cockatoo (*C. tenuirostris*, two subspecies)
Ducorp's cockatoo (*C. ducorps*)
Blue-eyed cockatoo (*C. ophthalmica*)
Greater Sulphur-crested cockatoo* (*C. galerita*, four subspecies)
Lesser Sulphur-crested cockatoo* (*C. sulphurea*, six subspecies)

Umbrella-crested, White-crested or Greater White-crested cockatoo* (*C. alba*)

Moluccan cockatoo* (*C. moluccensis*)

Leadbeater's cockatoo (*C. leadbeateri,* four subspecies)

Frequently Kept Cockatoo Species

Altogether, there are only eight cockatoo species that are usually available commercially. A detailed description of each of these species follows.

Rose-breasted or Roseate Cockatoo, or Galah

Eolophus roseicapillus (3 subspecies)

Description: Total length 13½ inches (35 cm).

Male: upper side gray, underside rose-red; forehead, crown, neck, and (recumbent) crest feathers pale pink, almost white; undertail coverts gray; tail underside gray-black; beak yellowish gray; legs gray; iris dark brown to black. Female: similar to male but iris red to red-brown.

Distribution: Entire interior of Australian continent.

Habitat: Primarily dry areas, but also other forms of climate and vegetation; frequently in the vicinity of artificially-created water areas, in parks and gardens.

Maintenance: Because they have been traditionally among the most expensive parrots rosies were usually kept as breeders. They are skillful fliers, even indoors. As aviary birds they are relatively undemanding and exceptionally climate-resistant.

Breeding: Often successful. In courtship the male struts up to the female, bows his head forward, and raises his crest. A brief chattering of the beak accompanies wooing. Before egg laying the females line the nest box with small branches and leaves. The clutch consists of three to four eggs, which are brooded by both parents taking turns for 25 days. After about seven weeks the young leave the nest box.

As Companions: Cautious to the point of sometimes being shy. Clear and distinct human mimicks. Rosies have a reputation for both gnawing less and screaming less loudly than other common companion cockatoos. Typically high energy, but occasionally tending to obesity.

Philippine or Red-vented Cockatoo

Cacatua haematuropygia

Description: Total length 12 inches (31 cm). Male: basic plumage color white; ear patch pale yellow; small recumbent crest with yellowish color at base of feathers; underwing coverts and underside of tail yellowish; rump plumage red with white margins; unfeathered eye ring white; beak gray-white; legs gray; iris black-brown. Female: similar to male, but iris red-brown to red.

Distribution: Philippine Islands including Palawan and the Sulu Islands.

Habitat: Primarily forests with primitive vegetation; only occasionally seeks open areas and wheat fields along the edges of forests for feeding.

Maintenance: Keeping the Philippine cockatoo is not apt to be problem-free. Young birds have a tendency to disturbances of plumage development during the first major molt (see Common Illnesses, page 46), which frequently results in death. It is necessary to be especially careful when choosing a bird to buy (see Choosing a Healthy Cockatoo, page 13). The voice of the Philippine cockatoo is quite tolerable and is usually heard in the morning and evening. Roomy aviaries with heated shelters are recommended for these extraordinary flyers. They have a tendency toward feather plucking in close quarters (or when kept singly).

Breeding: Successful only occasionally; the first successful breeding in the world was done by W. Eichelberger in 1974 in Switzerland. Philippine cockatoos are choosy when looking for a mate. During the brooding period the males become very aggressive, even toward their females, and can sometimes inflict serious wounds. The clutch consists of two to three eggs. The brooding period lasts about 30 days. After some 60 days the young leave the nest box.

Goffin's Cockatoo
Cacatua goffini

Description: Total length 12½ inches (32 cm). Male: basic plumage color white; bridle pink; small recumbent crest; undersides of wing and tail yellowish; unfeathered eye ring gray-white; beak whitish yellow; legs light gray; iris black. Female: similar to male except iris brown-red.

Distribution: Exclusively on Tanimbar Island off New Guinea.

Habitat: Primarily forest.

Maintenance: One of the smallest cockatoos, it appears not to be very popular among parrot fanciers; very little has been reported about it over the last ten years. Goffin's cockatoos offer no problems in maintenance and are undemanding. They can be wintered over in a dry, draft-free, slightly heated bird house. Nevertheless, Goffin's cockatoos have a strong need to gnaw and a relatively loud voice.

Breeding: Rarely successful; the first successful German attempt was made in 1978 by Th. Weise in Dortmund. These little cockatoos display rather inconspicuous courtship behavior, which is accompanied (in both sexes) by chattering of the beak. The clutch consists of two to three eggs. The brooding period runs 26 to 28 days. It is not known exactly when the young leave the nest box. Accounts on record range from 60 to 85 days.

As Companions: A cautious, reactionary bird with a tendency to form extreme and unpredictable bonds that can foster unwanted behaviors such as feather plucking. Often scream, even in the dark. Like other types of companion cockatoos, Goffin's cockatoos allowed to roam on the floor can easily develop a habit of attacking toes.

Bare-eyed Cockatoo or Little Corella
Cacatua sanguinea (2 subspecies)

Description: Total length 15½ inches (40 cm). Male and female: basic plumage color white with reddish tinges on forehead, crown, neck, and throat areas; small recumbent crest; blue-gray unfeathered eye ring; beak horn-colored to white; legs gray; iris in both sexes dark brown to black. Female is usually smaller than the male.

Distribution: The nominate form in eastern, northwestern, and northern Australia, the subspecies *C. sanguinea normantoni* in parts of southern New Guinea.

Habitat: Primarily dry inland areas; open country along river courses is favored, unbroken forests largely avoided. Like the Rose-breasted cockatoo, the Bare-eyed cockatoo has followed humankind into gardens and parks and sometimes inflicts great damage on grain-growing areas.

Two different Goffin's cockatoos.

Maintenance: Because Australia has banned the export of all plant and animal species since 1960, animals from the subspecies *C. sanguinea normantoni,* which stems from New Guinea, are more common in captivity.

Breeding: Although imported only in small numbers, breeding is often relatively successful. The largest breeding attempt to date was made by the San Diego (California) Zoo, which between 1929 and 1970 produced 103 young from a single pair—most of which were then hand-raised.

The clutch consists of two to three eggs. The length of brooding ranges from 21 to 24 days. The young leave the nest box after 45 to 50 days.

As Companions: Young birds quickly learn to imitate words. Bare-eyed cockatoos have extremely loud voices and a strong need to gnaw. Has a reputation for mischief. Can easily tend toward obesity.

Greater Sulphur-crested Cockatoo
Cacatua galerita (4 subspecies)

Description: Total length 19½ inches (50 cm). Male: basic plumage color white; ear spots—depending on subspecies—pale yellow to yellow; recurve crest, undersides of tail and wings yellow; unfeathered eye ring white; beak gray-black; legs gray; iris deep dark brown to black. Female: similar to male, but iris is reddish

The Moluccan cockatoo.

brown. The triton cockatoo *(C. galerita triton)* differs from all the other subspecies in that it has a blue, unfeathered eye ring.

Distribution: Northeastern and southern Australia, Tasmania, King Island, New Guinea, Aru Island.

Habitat: Open forested land, usually in the vicinity of water courses; occasionally also swampy areas and tropical rain forests.

Maintenance: After the Moluccan cockatoo, the Greater Sulphur-crested cockatoo is the largest of the common cockatoos. It has an outstanding need to gnaw and utters piercing screams. Aviary birds are robust and unde-manding. Except in the coldest of climates, they can even be wintered in unheated, but dry and draft-free, quarters.

Breeding: Often successful. Greater Sulphur-crested cockatoos exhibit impressive courtship behavior, with fanned tail feathers, erected crests, and jerky display movements. The clutch consists of two to three eggs. The brooding time lasts around 30 days (both sexes take turns brooding, during the day by the male and night by the female). The nestling period lasts around 85 days. Young birds feed indepen-dently in about 100 days.

As Companions: Famous screamers and chewers, the Greater Sulphur-crested cockatoos are often unsuited to apartments or other closely spaced dwellings.

A Lesser Sulfur-crested with its favorite ball.

Lesser Sulphur-crested Cockatoo

Cacatua sulphurea (6 subspecies)

Description: Total length 13¼ inches (34 cm). Male: basic plumage color white; round ear spots, recurve crest, undersides of wings, and tail yellow. Female: similar to male but iris turns brownish red after the third year. Of all six subspecies of the Lesser Sulphur-crested cockatoo, the Citron-crested cockatoo (*C. sulphurea citrinocristata*) is the most striking. Instead of the yellow markings it has orange ear spots and an orangey crest.

Distribution: Celebes (Sulawesi), Sunda Islands, several small islands of the Flores and the Java Seas.

Habitat: Open forest areas, occasionally unbroken forests and wheat-growing areas.

Maintenance: Most frequently kept in captivity of any of the cockatoo species; at one time they were particularly preferred as house pets, but today they are increasingly kept as pairs in the aviary. Lesser Sulphur-crested cockatoos need roomy quarters, for they are good fliers; they are more active than the Greater Sulphur-crested. Their tremendous beak strength requires a sturdily built aviary. Natural branches and little boards should be provided regularly to prevent boredom and to satsify their need to gnaw.

Breeding: Easiest to breed of all the cockatoos. Choosing mates sometimes turns out to be difficult, however, for it can happen that the male will be very aggressive toward the female and chase her through the aviary, often to the point of exhaustion, and also drive her away from the feeding place. It is wise, therefore, to provide escape possibilities and blinders for the protection of the female. Sometimes it will be necessary to change mates. The courtship is very impressive, with erected crest, spread tail, erect strutting, and jerky bowing, similar to that of the Greater Sulphur-crested cockatoo. The clutch consists of two to three eggs, which are brooded by both sexes. Brooding lasts about 24 days (in Citron-crested cockatoos 27 to 28 days). The nestling period takes eight to ten weeks. Young do not acquire the black beak until they are approximately seven months old.

As Companions: Famous screamers and chewers, even the smallest Lesser Sulphur-crested cockatoos may be unsuited to apartments. Mature males may be especially unpredictable biters.

Umbrella, White-crested, or Greater White-crested Cockatoo

Cacatua alba

Description: Total length 17½ inches (45 cm). Male: basic plumage color white; broad recurve crest white; unfeathered eye ring cream white; beak black; legs dark gray; iris dark brown to black. Female: similar to male, but iris red-brown.

Distribution: Moluccas Obi, Batjan, Soa-Siu (Tidore), and Ternate.

Habitat: Largely unknown; some authorities believe that the birds live in forests and around farmland in pairs or small groups.

Maintenance: Umbrella pairs must be kept only in roomy, sturdy quarters, for they are very loud and their beaks are strong enough to destroy everything. Aviary keeping is recommended, however; there the birds are relatively undemanding, but they do need a slightly warmed house for protection.

Breeding: The first successful breeding attempts were reported in the United States during the 1960s and 1970s; currently there are perhaps about ten breeding pairs in Germany. The courtship probably starts with the female. Before copulation she performs a kind of courtship dance in which she hops from one leg to the other. The clutch consists of an average of two eggs. Brooding lasts from 29 to 30 days. The nestling period extends for 80 to 100 days.

As Companions: Umbrella cockatoos are probably too loud and destructive for most apartments and closely spaced dwellings. Males can be as unpredictable as teenagers; females probably make better long-term companions.

Moluccan Cockatoo

Cacatua moluccensis

Description: Total length 21½ inches (55 cm). Male: basic plumage color white, often with pinkish tinge; with pink covert feathers covering a large orange-red recumbent crest; beak black; legs gray; iris black. Female: similar to male but iris can be deep brown.

Distribution: Moluccan Islands Seram, Saparua, and Haruku, introduced to Ambon Island.

Habitat: Forested areas near the coast, principally low areas and hilly country under 3,280 feet (1000 m); in small flocks.

Maintenance: The largest cockatoos available commercially. They are best maintained in pairs in an outdoor aviary at least 6 feet (2 m) wide and with plenty of opportunity for exercise and occupation. Some birds can even be kept on a climbing tree when their wing feathers are well clipped (see page 35).

Breeding: Rarely successful; five or six successful attempts have been reported in Germany in which chicks were reared by their parents. A number of Moluccan cockatoos have been hand-raised in Europe, England, and the United States. The sensitive nature of the bird, the difficulty in establishing a pair, the need for huge quarters, and the price of acquiring two birds considerably increase the difficulty of attempting to breed Moluccan cockatoos. The clutch usually consists of two to three eggs. The brooding period lasts 28 to 30 days. The nestling period extends for approximately 90 days.

As Companions: Their piercingly loud cries, destructive beak strength, and size, among other characteristics, make them difficult to keep as companions, especially in apartments and closely spaced dwellings. Moluccan cockatoos are very sensitive animals and can easily become feather pickers.

[1]Murphy, James J. *Cockatoos are Different Because They Have Crests,* White Mt. Bird Firm, Inc., 1998.

Another view of fun-loving Moluccans sharing a playful moment.

INFORMATION

Books

Athan, Mattie Sue. *Guide to the Well-Behaved Parrot,* Hauppauge, NY: Barron's Educational Series, Inc., 1993.

_____. *Guide to Companion Parrot Behavior,* Hauppauge, NY: Barron's Educational Series, Inc., 1993.

Bergman, Petra. *Feeding Your Pet Bird,* Hauppauge, NY: Barron's Educational Series, Inc., 1993.

Harrison, Greg J., CVM, and Harrison, Linda R., BS. *Clinical Avan Medicine and Surgery,* Philadelphia, PA: W.B. Saunders Company, 1986.

Jupiter, Tony and Parr, Mike. *Parrots: A Guide to Parrots of the World,* New Haven, CT: Yale University Press, 1998.

Murphy, James J. *Cockatoos Are Different Because They Have Crests,* Gilbert, PA: White Mountain Bird Farm, Inc., 1998.

Murphy, Kevin. *Training Your Parrot,* Neptune, NJ: T.F.H. Publications, Inc., 1983.

Ritchie, Harrison. *Avian Medicine: Principles and Application,* Lake Worth, FL: Wingers Publishing, Inc., 1994.

Vriends, Matthew, Ph.D. *Lories and Lorikeets,* Hauppauge, NY: Barron's Educational Series, Inc., 1992.

Organizations

American Federation of Aviculture
P. O. Box 56218
Phoenix, AZ 85079

Association of Avian Veterinarians
(561) 393-8901

British Columbia Avicultural Society
11784 - 9th Ave.
North Delta, B.C. V4C 3H6

Canadian Avicultural Society
32 Dronmore Ct.
Willowdale, Ontario M2R 2H5

Canadian Parrot Association
Pine Oaks R. R. #3
Catherines, Ontario L2R 6P9

The Gabriel Foundation
P. O. Box 11477
Aspen, CO 81612
(970) 923-1009

International Aviculturists Society
P.O. Box 2232
LaBelle, FL 33975

Oasis Parrot Sanctuary
P.O. Box 3104
Scottsdale, AZ 85271
(602) 265-6783

The Tropics Exotic Bird Refuge
Kannapolis, NC 28081
(704) 932-8041

World Parrot Trust
P. O. Box 34114
Memphis, TN 38184

Age, 14–15
Anatomy, 47
Appearance, 13–14
Aviary:
  bird's placement in, 25–26
  cleaning of, 35
  equipment for, 18–19
  outdoor, 22–23
  placement of, 19–20

Bare-eyed cockatoo, 8, 21, 71–72
Bathing pan, 19
Beak, 6, 34, 63
Behavior
  breeding, 55
  comfort, 63
  courtship, 55, 64
  display, 64
  managing of, 66
  social, 63
  threatening, 66
  types of, 62–64
Bird room, 17–18
Bird shelter
  bird's placement in, 25–26
  building of, 22–23
  cleaning of, 27
Black Palm cockatoo, 44
Bonding, 5
Breeders, 12
Breeding:
  brooding period, 55, 58
  diet for, 54
  overbreeding concerns, 53
  pairing, 54
  success in, 53–54
Brooding period, 55, 58–59, 61–62
Buying:
  considerations before, 7
  first days after, 25
  formalities of, 15
  health evaluations before, 13–14
  locations for, 12
  pair of birds, 11

Cage:
  cleaning of, 35
  equipment for, 18–19
  flight, 22–23, 27
  indoor, 17
  introducing bird to, 25–26
  placement of, 19–20

  selection of, 6
  size of, 17
  substrate for, 19
Calcium block, 19
Care measures, 34–35
Cats, 11
Characteristics, 5–6, 69–70
Children, 11
Citron cockatoo, 60
Claw trimming, 34
Climbing tree, 20–21
Companion, 7, 10
Copulation, 55, 66
Courtship, 55, 64

Dangers, 29–31
Diet. See also Food and feeding
  animal protein, 38–39
  for breeding, 54
  fruits, 37–38
  manufactured, 37
  minerals, 42
  vegetables, 37–38
  vitamins, 42–43
Dogs, 11
Drinking, 62

Eating, 62
Egg laying, 55, 58
Environment, 10–11
Exercises, 62–63, 67

Feather eating, 50–51
Feather plucking, 50–51
First aid, 45
Flight cage, 22–23, 27
Food and feeding. See also Diet
  guidelines for, 42
  inappropriate, 39
  quantity of, 42
  rearing, 39
  sprouted, 38
  for young birds, 59
Food dish, 18–19, 42
Free flight, 20
Fruits, 37–38

Gender determinations, 14
Goffin's cockatoo, 52, 57, 71–72
Greater Sulfur-crested cockatoo, 12, 24, 37, 56, 72–74

Greater White-crested cockatoo, 74–75

Hand-raising, 58–59
Hand-taming, 26
Hazards, 29–31
Health evaluations, 13–14
Housing. See also Aviary; Cage
  for breeding, 53
  evaluations of, 13
  for young birds, 59
Hygiene, 12

Illness:
  endoparasites, 46
  feather eating, 50–51
  feather plucking, 50–51
  intestinal inflammation, 46
  parrot fever, 51
  psittacine beak and feather disease, 51
  respiratory, 46, 50
Information sources, 77
Injuries, 35
Intestinal inflammation, 46

Leadbeater's cockatoo, 33
Leg band, 15
Lesser Sulfur-crested cockatoo, 12, 24, 37, 56, 73–74
Long-billed Corella cockatoo, 48

Mimicking, 6
Minerals, 42
Moluccan cockatoo, 49, 75

Natural habitat, 61–62
Nest box, 19, 54

Open perch, 20–21
Organizations, 77
Other birds, 11
Outdoors, 21

Pairing, 54
Parasites, 46
Parrot fever, 51
Parrots, 11
Perch, 18, 20
Pets, 11
Pet shop, 12

Philippine cockatoo, 70–71
Plants, 20
Playfulness, 5
Plumage, 5, 14–15
Poison dangers, 31
Poisoning, 46
Preening, 6, 55, 63, 66
Protective efforts, 53
Protein, 38–39
Psittacine beak and feather disease, 51
Psittacosis. See Parrot fever
Purchasing. See Buying

Respiratory illnesses, 46, 50
Rose-breasted cockatoo, 9, 32, 64, 68, 70

Sales contract, 15
Sanctuary, 12
Second cockatoo, 11, 27
Shelter. See Bird shelter
Showering, 34–35, 62–63
Sleeping, 62
Step-up practice, 67

"Talk," 26
Transportation, 45
Trimming:
  of beak, 34
  of claws, 34
  of wing feathers, 34–35

Umbrella cockatoo, 16, 28, 40, 74–75
Unweaned bird, 7, 39

Vegetables, 37–38
Veterinarian, 25, 45
Vitamins, 42–43

Water, 42
Water dish, 18–19
White-crested cockatoo, 74–75
Wing feathers, 34–35
Wounds, 35

Young birds:
  development of, 58
  food and feeding of, 39, 59
  hand-raising of, 58–59
  illustration of, 56–57

About the Authors

Werner Lantermann has been director of a private institute for parrot research in Oberhausen, Germany, since 1981. His specialty is the large parrots of South and Central America. He is the author of numerous articles in professional journals and successful books about parrotkeeping and breeding, among them Barron's *The New Parrot Handbook* and *Amazon Parrots*.

Susan Lantermann is a co-worker in the private institute for parrot research in Oberhausen, Germany, and co-author of numerous books about African and South American parrots.

Matthew Vriends, Ph.D. is a Dutch-born biologist and orinthologist who has written over 100 books in three languages on birds and other animals. His detailed works on parrots are highly respected in the field.

Cover Photos

All cover photos (front, back, inside front, and inside back) by Joan Balzarini.

Photo Credits

Schweiger: page 64
Skogstad: page 65
All other photos by Joan Balzarini.

Additional Illustrations

Tanya M. Heming-Vriends: pages 22–23.

Important Note
While every effort has been made to ensure that all information in this text is accurate, up-to-date, and easily understandable, we cannot be responsible for unforeseen consequences of the use or misuse of this information. Poorly social-ized or unhealthy parrots may be a danger to humans in the household. Escaped non-native species represent an environmental threat in some places. Outdoor release or unrestricted outdoor flight is condemned by the ethical parrot keeper.

English translation © copyright 2000, 1989 by Barron's Educational Series, Inc.
© Copyright 1988 by Gräfe und Unzer GmbH, Munich, Germany.
Original title of the German book is *Kakadus*.
Translated from the German by Elizabeth D. Crawford.

All inquiries should be addressed to:
Barron's Educational Series, Inc.
250 Wireless Boulevard
Hauppauge, NY 11788
http://www.barronseduc.com

ISBN-13: 978-0-7641-1037-5
ISBN-10: 0-7641-1037-3

Library of Congress Catalog Card No. 99-86987

Library of Congress Cataloging-in-Publication Data
Lantermann, Werner, 1956–
   [Kakadus. English]
   Cockatoos: acclimation, care, feeding, sickness, and breeding : special chapter, Understanding cockatoos / Werner and Susanne Lantermann ; consulting editor, Matthew M. Vriends ; with color photographs by well-known animal photographers and drawings by Fritz W. Köhler.—2nd ed.
      p. cm.
   Includes bibliographical references (p.   ).
   ISBN 0-7641-1037-3
   1. Cockatoos. I. Lantermann, Susanne.
II. Vriends, Matthew M., 1937– . III. Title.
   SF473.C63 L3513   2000
   636.6'865—dc21   99-86987
                                               CIP

Printed in China
19 18 17 16 15 14 13